Can You Run Your Business With Blood, Sweat, and Tears? Volume II

Can You Run Your Business With Blood, Sweat, and Tears? Volume II

Sweat

Stephen Elkins-Jarrett
Nick Skinner

BEP BUSINESS EXPERT PRESS

Can You Run Your Business With Blood, Sweat, and Tears? Volume II: Sweat
Copyright © Business Expert Press, LLC, 2018.

First published in 2018 by
Business Expert Press, LLC
222 East 46th Street, New York, NY 10017
www.businessexpertpress.com

ISBN-13: 978-1-94858-038-0 (paperback)
ISBN-13: 978-1-94858-039-7 (e-book)

Business Expert Press Entrepreneurship and Small Business Management Collection

Collection ISSN: 1946-5653 (print)
Collection ISSN: 1946-5661 (electronic)

Cover and interior design by S4Carlisle Publishing Services
Private Ltd., Chennai, India

First edition: 2018

10 9 8 7 6 5 4 3 2 1

Printed in the United States of America.

Dedication

For Eddie and Leia

STRATEGY

WHAT IF

EVIDENCE

ACTION

TIMINGS

Abstract

What does it take to successfully lead and manage a business or a team? Management consultant and HR specialist Stephen-Elkins Jarrett and organizational development consultant Nick Skinner share their combined experience of how mastery of 15 key areas can help you drive your business, team, or even yourself to success. Presented using the acronym of BLOOD, SWEAT, and TEARS, this book, presented in three volumes, aligns some established models with common sense to give a practical view with tools and tips gained over years of working across different industries and sectors. At the heart of the book is the fascinating study of behavior, discussed through the SPECTRUM model of behavior, showing how by treating others in the way that they want to be treated, we can engage, develop, and lead them to achieve meaningful goals.

Keywords

behavior, development, HR, human resources, leadership, management, performance, SPECTRUM, strategy, team, teamwork

Contents

Foreword

Blood, Sweat, and Tears

Elkins-Jarrett & Skinner

Stephen and Nick have packed a huge amount into three volumes. Their years of business consulting experience is evident as they make every element wholly understandable and immensely practical—this is not a book about business theory; it is a book to be put into immediate action.

Using the acronym B-L-O-O-D S-W-E-A-T-and-T-E-A-R-S, they consider 16 areas of importance in business success (the "and" is an important area, hence 16) and within these incorporate aspects as disparate as time management, presentation skills, work–life balance, vision, and performance management, in addition to the chapter titles such as Brand, Leadership, Opportunities, and so forth using illustrations from areas as diverse as Psychology and Star Wars.

Running through the book is the recurring theme of understanding and appreciating human behavior in its many facets. They expound "Spectrum" behavioral psychometric, which fits with the themes of their book—approachable, easy to understand, and practical. All other Jungian models would also work, but I agree with them that Spectrum's simplicity enhances the ability to apply the learning effortlessly and across all cultures.

Throughout the chapters, they make use of well-known, tried-and-tested theories including Tuckman, Maslow, Kotter, and Hersey & Blanchard—only models and structures that have stood the test of time rather than any that are likely to be in vogue today and forgotten tomorrow. Within these, they give their own adaptations and developments driven by decades of management consulting experience, which make them more practical and more applicable.

If you are looking for a book that covers a wide range of criteria for business success and is eminently readable, down-to-earth, practical, and developed through the crucible of decades of experience, *Blood, Sweat, and Tears* is a wise choice.

Stephen Berry

MBA, MSc, BSc(Hons), FCMA, CGMA, ACIB, DipFS, PgD

Author of *Strategies of the Serengeti* (2006; 2nd ed., 2010)

and

Teach Yourself Strategy in a Week (2012; 2nd ed., 2016)

Introduction to Blood, Sweat, and Tears

"I have nothing to offer except blood, sweat and tears!" paraphrased from a speech given to the UK houses of parliament in the dark days of 1940 by Prime Minister Sir Winston Churchill.

Hello and welcome to *Blood, Sweat & Tears*! Why did we write it? What is it all about? And who the heck are these guys anyway?

Stephen's Story

My story is that I have been working since I was 16. My background is strange but has given me an insight into the commercial world that others don't get. I did not have a classic educational background. My parents divorced when I was 11. My father was in sales and my mother a sports teacher and legal secretary. At 16 my mother said leave school and go to work, we need the money. I trained as a chef, day release at Slough College, near Heathrow airport, I left after I had completed my OND and HND (Ordinary and Higher National Diplomas) to work with my father in the construction industry. I qualified in NFBPM at Diploma level. At the same time, I was involved in Amateur Dramatics. While in a play, I was approached by a director who asked me if I fancied quitting my job to be his personal assistant and learn his trade from the bottom. He was a Coopers & Lybrand Management Consultant, now running his own business. This was a single act of kindness that changed my world forever.

I went to night school to do my A levels, did a distance learning Degree with UEL in Industrial Psychology—now called Organizational. Then qualified in Psychometrics, Life Coaching, NLP, CBT, did a advanced diploma in organizational psychology at Oxford learning, and then finally got my Masters in Organizational Psychology just a few years ago.

Parallel to this I worked full time for Mike at Manskill Associates, watching, learning, listening, and delivering soft skills training, facilitated workshops, strategy workshops, leadership development, management and supervisory training and coaching. I also joined the CIPD and learned everything I could about HR and worked in HR departments as an interim for some great HR directors such as Julie Sutton and Talent Directors such as Joanne Rye. I worked as an interim HR director, HR manager, Employee relations manager, caseworker, a TUPE project manager, change, takeovers, mergers, and acquisitions. I saw and learned more from this strange and unusual journey through the commercial world than I would have done with a "proper job" as my wife calls it and in a traditional career along the way. I worked in the fields of catering, hospitality, healthcare, pharmaceutical, scientific institutions, and laboratories. I worked in construction, property, IT, finance, banking, FMCG, utilities, high-voltage power stations, supermarkets, motor industry, and several others, delivering soft skills training, group facilitation, coaching, team work, team building and more. I worked in the biggest and the smallest and everything in between and one thing remained constant for me—it is all the same. When recruiters look for someone with managerial experience in a certain industry, any manager could learn the new job and man management skills remain a constant; 80 percent is behaviors and 20 percent technical skills and knowledge and you can learn this bit as you go. Richard Branson said, "If anyone asks you if you can do this job, say yes and then learn it as you go." He has always done this.

Nick's Story

My story is almost the opposite; raised in Hertfordshire I scrapped the grades needed to do a first degree before taking a graduate job providing business and project accounting support to scientists. This was the late 1980s and the UK was still reeling from the impacts of Thatcherism, where large swaths of the UK infrastructure that had traditionally been operated using public money were being forced down a route that made them think more commercially. The reaction to the kind of externally and politically induced change created an organizational stress that taught me a lot. I realized quickly that while finance was important there was more to business than the accountants' view. Hence, I shifted away from finance and into broader business commercial management, completing an MBA with distinction in 1997 from the University of Hertfordshire and then shifting my career to London to work in the field of commercializing intellectual property, working as a business administrator for a spin-out company commercializing breakthroughs in cancer technology, developing plans for seed funds, and managing a large network of technology transfer stakeholders. Again, in this role I was providing commercial and business support to some very clever scientists. I moved back into agricultural sciences in 1999, working on business plans and change programs in that sphere for the next 13 years. It was a long time, but there were so many projects and exciting new businesses being developed that it was really more like four or five different jobs. Certainly, by the time I moved on from there I had earned my projects management wings, acting as the leader of a number of change programs which (mostly) went according to plan. There were some car crashes of course, but they got fewer, so I must have been getting better! Sometime while there I attended an eye-opening training program and came across some very bright cookies doing organizational development at Roffey Park. My training with these guys made me finally realize that what really goes on in business is a human interaction, and that to get great outcomes in business all you needed was great humans. Then it all started to fall in place. Great business outcomes are about great people, so if all humans are great this should be easy, right? Wrong! There's so much that we humans create and fantasize about and are scared of that prevents us from being at our best. I strongly believe that organizations that can remove these blocks and find a proper level of human connection can build trust, and once you have trust then you can really start to go places. I took an MSc in organizational and people development through Roffey Park and in 2012 backed my learning with the establishment of Poppyfish People Development, fulfilling a career dream of helping business capitalize on the potential of the human in the system and engaging in client work across multiple industries and coming across Steve Jarrett and his SPECTRUM model in 2013. As opposites attract we make a good team.

Coming Together

We met when a mutual friend and client, Ian Cresswell, a people-focused leader to whom we are both indebted, intuitively thought we would work well together in his organization. We did. Nick is more cautious and careful, methodical, analytical, and checks everything, and Stephen, dives in, cracks on, and says, "Everything will be alright in the end, if it is not alright it is not the end!" (Indian Proverb). Stephen thinks getting stuck in is the answer and Nick knows that to reflect and think about it first often gets a better outcome. Nick acts as the brake to Stephen's accelerator pedal and on average we work off each other well. Like many relationships the only challenges come when we both want to steer. We both believe in the power of dreams and that positivity and energy really count for something.

Our work together has been varied, challenging, but always rewarding, working as coaches, consultants, trainers, facilitators, and leaders of learning and behavior change for many individuals, teams, and businesses. In a nutshell, we help our clients align people performance with organization performance. We do this in many different industry sectors, including technical services, information technology, scientific research, start-ups, and construction. We don't spend much on marketing; instead, our growth has been through word of mouth and personal recommendation. We think that is important. It's part of our own brand.

We are guided by the simple principle that the best people build the best businesses. In a world increasingly driven by technical development and big data, workplaces remain a human environment. The performance of your business depends massively upon the talents, motivations, and behaviors of the people that work within it.

We want to see those people at their best, in a space where their talents shine.

To work with us is to recognize that each of us has our own dreams, aspirations, and desires, and that if we can tap into this rich vein of motivation then we can all fly. Our motives for writing this book are to capture some of the "common sense" activities that we think make a difference to how businesses perform. Most of what you will read here is not rocket science, but it is hopefully practical and resonates enough with your own experiences to allow you to feel confident and capable at making great things happen. It's a chance for us to share what we have learnt through the blood, sweat, and tears of our work, and hope that you find the content rewarding.

Blood, Sweat, and Tears

Blood, Sweat, and Tears is a simple to follow trilogy of books with most of the advice you could need to develop, grow, and succeed as a manger or leader in any team or business from a one-man self-employed person to a large enterprise. The ideas in this book have come about after many years of consulting practice—working with the great, the good (and even the bad). From seeing businesses fail and learning from their mistakes through to businesses that did great things and were successful the authors have picked up the best practices and principles that guide success. This book attempts to share our learning. The principles, ideas, and ways of thinking that are outlined in these pages will help to focus your thinking with regard to self-development, team development, and business development.

According to Bloomberg, 8 out of 10 entrepreneurs who start businesses fail within the first 18 months. A whopping 80 percent crash and burn after having the chance to send out only one lot of corporate Christmas cards. But why? The reasons that businesses fail are painful inasmuch as many of them are easily avoided.

At the surface level the primary reason businesses fail is that they run out of cash. But the reasons for that are deeper than apparent shallowness of the cash drawer. In our combined lives as consultants we have seen plenty, advised many, and been ignored by lots!

How can you avoid these failures? Only through the application of blood, sweat, and tears.

We have created BLOOD, SWEAT, and TEARS as an acronym for all the things that you can do that will help to drive success; setting out attitudes, behaviors, and practices that you can follow to help you achieve your and your company's goals. The ideas are developed throughout the following pages, with each letter of the acronym given its own chapter.

The acronym explained:

Book One

BLOOD is the life source of your success:

B stands for **BRAND**: Can you build the right brand for you and your business and demonstrate alignment between the two?

L stands for **LEADERSHIP**: Do you have the right skills to understand the needs of others and get the best out of yourself and your team?

O stands for **OPPORTUNITIES**: Can you manage the process of generating leads and prospects and take advantages of the opportunities that will grow your business?

O stands for **OUTCOMES**: Are you focusing on the right outcomes to hit your goals? How do you set goals and objectives?

D is for **DECISIONS**: Can you make the right decisions that lead to success?

Book Two

SWEAT are the exercises that you should constantly focus on.

S stands for **STRATEGIC DIRECTION**: Do you have the right vision, mission, strategy, and structure for your business to succeed?

W stands for **WHAT IF?** Do you know what to do in those "What If . . ." moments? Can you and your team be resilient or forward thinking enough to take steps to avoid confusion and chaos in a fast-changing world?

E stands for **EVIDENCE:** Can you find the evidence to back your intuition? What can you do to get the information you need to act for the best?

A stands for **ACTION**: Can you overcome the urge to procrastinate and take action when you need to?

T stands for **TIME:** Can you get your timings right and manage everything you have to do in a way that keeps you in control?

Don't forget "and": don't forget yourself and enjoyment and quality time and family and friends, etc.

Book Three

TEARS are the things that will refresh and reward you.

T stands for **TRAINING**: Are you training the right people in the right way—the essential tool that makes you ready to cope with the demand of tomorrow? Train people all the time and so they can leave—then treat them so they don't want to!

E is for **ENCOURAGEMENT**: To get the best out of others you must know what drives and motivates them. Can you give encouragement to others and know where to find your own?

A stands for **ANNOUNCEMENTS**: DO you announce the important things in the right way? How can you present for maximum impact?

R stands for **REVIEW**: Do you take time to reflect and review the past with an eye on the future? Take time at each step of the way to look back what you have achieved, what you can learn from it, and how this can help you for future planning.

S stands for **SUCCESS**: Can you deliver success for you, your team, and your business? How will you know you are succeeding and what to do next? Taking time to enjoy your successes has a narcotic effect, leaving you wanting more!

Our experience tells us that this is what makes a difference in successful organization. If you get it right the benefits can be stunning. Here's what happens if you get it wrong:

If you cannot identify or build your BRAND then you'll be faced with confused customers and staff who don't really know what the business (or you if you are the brand) stands for. You'll have to accept that others will define it for you.

If you do not develop the right LEADERSHIP skills you will create anxiety and frustration for others and increase the propensity for false starts and you will have to accept that people will be frustrated. You will start to lose people, starting with the best ones first.

If you fail to act on OPPORTUNITIES then you can expect finances to take a direct hit. The implications of this are obvious. While this is playing out you will generate anxiety for people who will realize that the writing is on the wall.

If you fail to identify the right OUTCOMES then people do the wrong thing. False starts happen and people get frustrated and confused. You cannot track progress. Tasks never finish. Morale drops. People leave. And so do customers.

If you struggle with DECISIONS then you can expect people to get frustrated and for confusion to reign. Lack of decision making provokes anxiety and slows your business down.

If you fail to define and communicate a STRATEGIC DIRECTION then chaos abounds. Your business becomes a lawless territory without guidance or a moral compass. People make up their own strategy and resist your efforts to pull them away from that because they do not know any better. You will never have buy in and without buy in you will be in a state of constant confusion. You will also be handing over control to the micro-managers.

If you fail to spot and train yourselves for the WHAT IF . . . moments then you will create anxiety as people will not feel equipped to deal with change and you will be left behind by the world. You also risk jeopardizing your business by reducing its resilience to the point where the slightest wave or market tremor could threaten its existence.

If you fail to secure EVIDENCE for changes you will cause frustration and run the risk of a number of false starts where you thought you were doing the right thing but, as it turns out, you are not. Oops. More prework and evidence might have helped. You'll also have egg on your face and could have just cost the business lots of money.

If you fail to take ACTION you will condemn your business or project to the scrapheap of time. The road to hell is paved with good intentions, so they say. So sort out your project plan and make it happen.

If you fail to get your TIMINGS right you will create inefficiencies and frustration and will probably lose money. Tasks will slip. And if you ask people to do what they see as the wrong thing at the wrong time, you will encounter resistance. Resistance is not futile, that's why we do it.

If you fail to TRAIN your people then your plans will be sabotaged by people who cannot do what you ask of them and who will not be able to grow themselves at a rate that allows them to deliver any growth to your business. People will be frustrated and will not feel important. Good people will leave while the less able struggle. As the old cliché goes: What if we train our people and they leave? Well, what if we don't train them and they stay?

Failure to ENCOURAGE people leads to alienation at work and development and strategic goals not being met. In addition, negativity will seep into the workplace and will be visible to customers. A negative team is a poor performing team. You also run the risk of sabotage, where people dig their heels in to actively prevent and delay progress (yes, it does happen!).

If you fail to ANNOUNCE what you are doing then you risk people putting their own reasons behind your motives. Nobody likes surprises and when people see the action but without knowing the reasons they have no chance to buy in, no chance to support or even realize what is going on. This creates resistance and can even promote fear as people often fantasize about losing their jobs.

If you fail to REVIEW then you are condemning yourself to repeating the same old mistakes again and again. Doing the same thing time after time and expecting a different outcome each time is a first definition of madness.

And if you fail to SUCCEED then celebrate small wins (because they will always be there) and keep trying, keep working, and think about which of the other 14 areas you needed to work at.

What about the "And?"

But what about that small conjunctive in the middle? The word "and." The word "and" is the glue that effortlessly ties everything together. It gives the three words meaning. Without the word "and" the three words BLOOD, SWEAT, TEARS appear nothing more than a list. But when we bring in the conjunctive "and" the three suddenly have cumulated impact, allowing the three to come together in a more powerful way. So, the "and" is more than just a word, it actually means something and pulls the concept together.

To this end we have devoted a chapter to the "and." So, what is it? In our view the "and" is the personal strength, power, and dedication that you will bring to your working world when you are at your best. The "and" includes your own metal health and physical well-being, it includes looking after your family and those around you and finding equal space in your life for all things.

So, read on. Challenge your mind to think creatively about how you can embed these ideas into your everyday thinking, thinking that will help you to define your vision and identify your product, price it correctly, take it to market, get business, make a profit, keep your customers wanting more, motivate and inspire your staff, delight your suppliers, reward your stakeholders and your loved ones, and give you a sense of satisfaction and delight in who you are and what you have achieved.

Our Methods

Throughout this book we employ some old techniques tried and tested since the ancient Greeks and developed further by a multitude of respected gurus, psychologists, organizational development theorists, coaches, management consultants, and successful businessmen and women from around the world. But we also give you new ideas and our latest thinking on some blended approaches which we have used and which we know work. We will give you war stories of where things didn't work and companies got it so wrong—and compare these to where they got it so right and share that best practices with you, giving you the best chance to set up and run your business or team successfully. We will introduce you to some models to help you conceptualize some of the more important areas.

How you use this book is up to you. You can read the book cover to cover in chapter order or jump directly to the area where you need help today and use it as a standalone chapter without the rest of the book holding you! So, if you just want to target specific areas then of course you can.

We hope very much that you enjoy BLOOD, SWEAT, and TEARS and that you can use it to fuel a wonderful success story.

Steve Elkins-Jarrett and Nick Skinner
London
April 2018

CHAPTER 1

S Is for Strategic Direction

Have You Set a Great Strategy to Develop Your Business?

*"In strategy, it is important to see distant things as if they were close,
and to take a distanced view of close things"*
—Miyamoto Musashi, legendary Japanese swordsman

Take a deep breath. In this chapter we are going to cover some of the most fundamental aspects of strategic management and direction. We will shine a light on such terms as vision, mission, values, structure, goals, behavior and culture. Each of these areas is a whole book in its own right, yet over the next few pages we will try to capture the headline perspective on these subjects that will help you make sure that you can formulate the best strategic direction for your business or team.

It goes without saying that any business must have strategic direction. In simple terms strategy addresses that most fundamental question: where are you trying to get to? How and why? What is it you want to achieve?

In Lewis Carroll's book *Alice in Wonderland*, Alice talks to the Cheshire cat:

Alice: "Would you tell me, please, which way I ought to go from here?"
The Cheshire Cat: "That depends a good deal on where you want to get to."
Alice: "I don't much care where."
The Cheshire Cat: "Then it doesn't much matter which way you go."

Alice: "... So long as I get somewhere."

The Cheshire Cat: "Oh, you're sure to do that, if only you walk long enough."

We have found so many businesses, even big ones, where the CEO, MD, and senior Directors know as much about strategy as Alice does. In short, they have no idea where they are going. We have actually worked for companies where the senior team does not even have nor want a strategy, a business plan, and certainly does not want to reveal it to their employees.

Morale dropped, people left, and they replaced them with cheaper, less qualified, and less experienced people and so the profits fell. What did they do? Make redundancies! These redundancies of course hit lower-level staff, the fee earners, and when we told the Leadership team and owners about the crazy nature of what was happening they sacked us too! The employees even asked for 2 years running—can we please have an annual conference so that you can tell us where we are going and what the plan is? The directors said No! The main work being done by the employees was creating a new CV and searching for a new job.

If this is true, then how can employees begin to know what needs to be done to get them there? Even in businesses where the Directors do know their strategy and vision, what we often see is that they set it behind closed doors and never tell anyone. The business plan, a mysterious document that is rumored to contain the answers to all business problems and challenges, is sometimes never actually committed to paper and seldom widely circulated. The normal reason stated for this is commercially sensitive information, but it's also sometimes because the board don't really know where they are going and are too scared to admit it. Humans do not like working in conditions of uncertainty. It's hard to commit to and communicate a plan in a volatile world, and it's hard to find your way at work in a job when you don't know where you are supposed to be going. Imagine working in a factory, and every day at 6 am you get up and at 7 am you start your 8-hour shift with 2 breaks and a lunch, weekends off and your annual holiday, you know the company you work for makes cars, but you have no idea what the lever does that you pull every 30 seconds that makes four nuts. How motivated and engaged are you? Now add that the CEO has engaged with you and all of your fellow workers and you have been trained to understand that the four nuts you produce hold the engine in place. Now add to that the company wants to ask you about how you think improvements could be made and finally add the fact that the CEO informs you that there is a brand new vehicle coming out and it is going to be made here, and that you will be a part of the team that creates the dream of an all-new electric vehicle, the first of its kind. This simple employee has not had any money spent on him, his wages have not gone up, nor does the secret that he now bears endanger the business but he is engaged, motivated, and keen to succeed. There is a pottery in Cornwall where every employee puts their name on the item as they process it, so that the customer can see who made it, painted it, and fired it. This also adds accountability as you will know the person who made the mistake! Therefore, allowing everyone to know your strategy is important; people generally want to be involved and have ownership, engagement, and feel connected to the man or woman at the top, even if they are collecting garbage, sweeping the street, or producing four nuts. In the Second World War, I had an uncle Kenneth Robison who flew Spitfires; he signed up when he was still 17, flew many missions, but just after his 21st birthday he was involved in a strategic meeting. His commanding officer gathered all his pilots together and said, "We need to do a daylight raid on Beuthen. But we cannot protect the bombers at low level and ensure they hit this very important strategic target." He went on to explain the strategic importance of the mission that the bombers would fly, the value of the raid to the war effort and to the security and future of their country, their homes, and their family. He explained that all other approaches to achieve the required result were impractical or had already failed. He told them that to attack would require resolve, courage, and sacrifice and provided some information on how the dangerous mission might be undertaken. For a moment after this briefing, the room was quiet. The strategy had been communicated. Apparently, the fighter pilots now knowing the strategic importance of this target all volunteered to escort the bombers across the English Channel all the way to the target and all the pilots knew it was a one-way ticket for them. They only had fuel to get there, not back again. He wrote to my grandmother sending his 21st birthday present of a golf watch back to her with the simple words—"I won't be needing this anymore." To get someone to buy in to your strategy to such an extent that they would willingly volunteer to help you carry it out means you have engaged and motivated to the point that they are prepared to die for it. So, when big companies arrogantly and secretly build a strategy in the board room with an elite set of directors and do not tell the stakeholders what they are doing and why, how can they ever be motivated to helping the company achieve it? How can the targets and goals be set if failure is more likely than success? Fire the emotion that sits inside people. Paint them a vision of what the future success looks like.

Vision is slightly more straightforward than strategy. Most people in a business can tell you broadly what the business is trying to achieve (i.e., it's vision and mission) but as for strategy, the all-important "how," well that is often far less clear. Therefore, the employee "journey" in pursuit of that strategy can be a sometimes confusing, and therefore disempowering, one.

Staff don't know what to do for the best. Imagine sitting on a train leaving London and heading for Leeds, when after an hour or so the driver decides to change routes, alter the signaling plans, and go to Manchester. How soon would the passengers in the last carriage find out? Probably on arrival when they see the signs. This is how many businesses treat their employees. They tell them little or nothing or such limiting

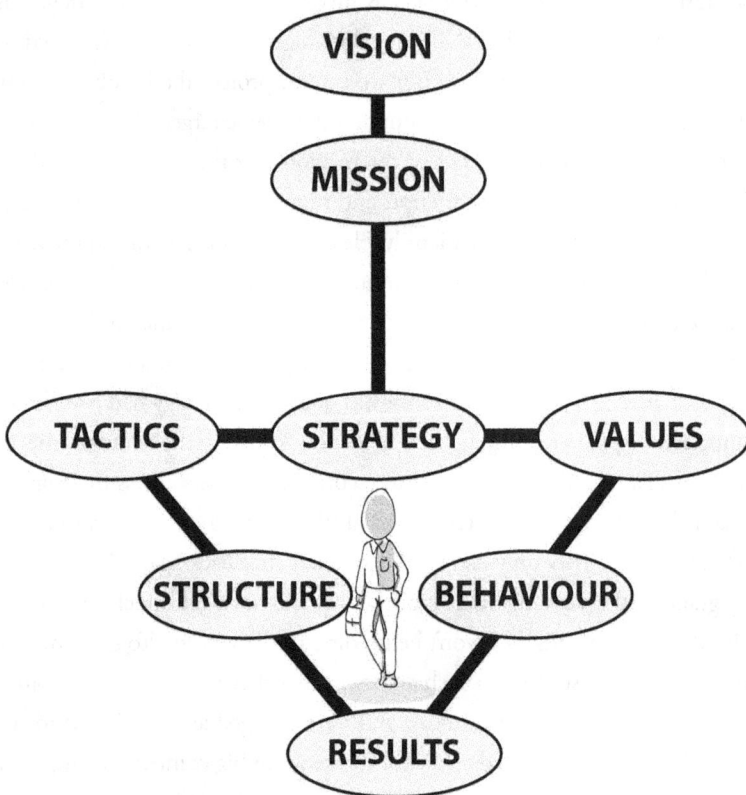

Vision, mission, strategy and culture

information that the employees make the rest up and there begins low staff morale and whispers around coffee machines.

Why would any senior leadership team keep secrets from their employees? Imagine a great leader in a battle not telling his officers and the officers not telling the soldiers what they were trying to achieve before they started—it would be chaotic at best and at the worst cost more lives. Much of this comes down to trust, and fear. In truth these two feelings shape much of our behavior, and in these situations, it is a brave foot soldier that makes a decision without first referring it up the line for approval.

Vision and Mission

Vision and Mission are the guiding lights that will influence your strategy, shining a reference point for decision making. When faced with two options, you take the one that moves you closer to your goal. Simple really, and very, very empowering. The VISION for the organization should be a simple but powerful statement describing the ideal future or what the organization wants to become. The best visions align the whole organization around a common future and inspire individuals to perform with passion. The MISSION provides focus and direction for how the organization will achieve its vision. It describes the purpose of the company—what it does and who it does it for. The mission might also state a number of specific GOALS. These are the targets toward which the organization is working. They will often include timeframes and metrics. Some examples of a Mission/Vision Statements include:

"To make a contribution to the world, by making tools for the mind, that advance humankind" (1980 Steve Jobs Apple)

"We work hard every day to make American Express the world's most respected brand" (American Express)

"It is our goal to be earth's most customer-centric company, where customers can find and discover anything they might want to buy online" (Amazon)

"To be the ultimate house of luxury, defining style and creating desire, now and forever!" (Chanel)

"To refresh the world in mind, body and spirit. To inspire moments of optimism and happiness through our brands and actions. To create value and make a difference" (Coca Cola)

"To give people the power to share and make the world more open
and connected" (Facebook)

"To organise the world's information and make it universally acces-
sible and useful." (Google)

"To bring inspiration and innovation to every athlete in the world—if
you have a body you are an athlete!" (Nike)

Possibly the most famous mission statement of all time came from the
mouth of President John F Kennedy who stated in 1961 that it was his
intention that ". . .*before this decade is out, to land a man on the moon and
return him safely to earth.*"

Your vision, mission, and values will be a heavy influencer of your
brand. Revisit the work and thinking that you did in that chapter from
the first volume in this trilogy; "Blood" (and if you haven't read that
book yet then put it on your reading list). How does your brand sit with
your mission statement? Hopefully the two are congruent. The more
aligned they are the more successful you are likely to be.

Culture

Every business has a culture and this culture operates at many levels. And
although we have all experienced culture it is actually quite a difficult thing
to define. But on the basis that simple is good, let's just stick with culture as
being "how we do things in this business." From a leader's perspective culture is quite hard to get right. For instance, a Booz Allen survey noted that
96 percent of people believe culture change is needed in their organization
in some form and 51 percent felt that their business needed a major culture
overhaul. When culture misaligns with strategy, then problems are more
likely to be seen. It's a tough thing to get right. From an organizational perspective culture is apparent at three levels (see diagram). On the one level we
have *desired culture*: how we want the business to be seen by its stakeholders.
Below that we have the *actual culture*: how all employees from the directors
to the janitor and everyone in between actually treat each other on a day-
to-day basis at work—what it's really like to work in the business. And then
finally we have the *perceived culture* of how the outside world perceives the
business. This is the stakeholders' view, from the outside in, including suppliers, rivals, shareholders, investors, the press, media, social media too. The

desired culture often speaks of brand ideals and living the values. The actual culture shows how well the organization is at really living those values, and the perceived culture is whether or not people see what you want them to see (remember the neighbor's dog with the "I don't bite" sign from our chapter on Brand on the first volume of this trilogy). Managing culture is tough. You prod it here and it moves over there, but maybe not immediately. Yet it is crucially important to how your business or team runs. Edgar Schein once wrote "*The only thing of real importance that leaders do is create and manage culture.*" Just as with branding, if these three cultures of desired, actual, and perceived are in alignment then you have a congruent business, but if they are different, even if just one is out of alignment with the rest, then your business will not be congruent culturally and you will need to take immediate action to address this. Imagine if your shopping experience was way out of line with how that retailer portrayed themselves externally. Or if the retailer carried out some practices which went against your values or beliefs. What if the retailer's vision, mission, and values, brand and slogan all said, "we are the best quality manufacturer and high end branded product, it is expensive and exclusive", yet in the written media or on social media you read that they were using sweat shops in India to make their items and they paid staff $1 a day to work 15 hours a day and source their raw materials from the cheapest suppliers they can find? You may find it hard to buy from them again. But if they actual said "our items are the cheapest and made from the cheapest materials, from the cheapest supplier, using the cheapest labour all to keep prices down, and for us it all about giving you the item at the lowest price," you may not mind that the staff and animals are being poorly treated and may choose to still buy the item. Alternatively, the company could do something about the conditions for the staff, suppliers, and animals and thus realign the perceived culture. Ever wondered how some businesses sell their products so cheaply? Look behind the scenes and into the actual culture and you may see some practices that would surprise you. The newspapers and lobby groups love these stories.

I once sat on a flight and once onboard was told that it was the maiden flight with passengers and as such got a welcome pack. The first sentence was, "This plane was made from the cheapest materials available in the world and as such we can offer low cost flights". My colleague and I, who were starting to feel somewhat worried at this revelation, then asked: "so you used the cheapest engines, cheapest navigation system and radar?"

"Well no," she said, "but it was value for money—we got a great deal." The two things are not the same. The desired value was "value" and what we experienced was "cheap." I do not want to go on a plane made from the cheapest materials, but I am happy to fly in a plane made from the best value for money. The welcome pack was withdrawn and reissued on all subsequent flights as "value for money!"

Strategy

The STRATEGY is the way that the organization intends to go about achieving its goals. As in the Cheshire Cat example, if you don't know where you are going, then any road may take you there. Having a clear vision and mission gives an unequivocal view of the ambitions of the organization and toward which the organization can build a demanding goal and select appropriate strategies. Sometimes these demanding goals are known as BHAGS (pronounced beehags—big hairy ambitious goals); a number of different strategies are likely to be employed, each with the aim of supporting the organizational goals, mission, and vision. Very often strategy is set from the top-down. But smart organizations are engaging with employees and managers across the business to input into the overall business strategy from the bottom-up, the middle up and down, and the top-down. Most organizations ignore the bottom and the middle and start just from the top, and then stop. They impose bizarre key performance indicators (KPIs) from the top-down, then dictate budgets, which tend to be a guess of what is required based on last year's figures and tinkered with, and then tell the whole business to just get on with it. Sound familiar? Then every month or 3 months they criticize the teams for not achieving their targets at the dreaded board meetings—which tend to look backward, filled with reports of what has gone wrong and then stumbling to find a way forward based on the past month or quarters performance.

We believe in a more engaging approach to strategy. Instead, what we do is get a wider group of stakeholders to have a say and to create their vision and strategy through interactive workshops and talking to them. This idea came about when many years ago I was walking around the shop floor of a large business in London, discussing a troublesome issue that we were helping with when the CEO asked me, "How do you solve this business problem we have?" As a young, fresh-faced consultant I felt put on the spot by this powerful businessman but was just stealing myself for an answer when a man pushing a broom nearby looked up and said, "Why don't you just ask the person who does that job what they think is the answer!" And there was born an approach that we have tried to take ever since, which is if you want answer to any problem ask the person who does that job how to solve it! The person close to the issue often has an opinion on what could or should be done, so why not ask them what needs to happen? It's not rocket science, but something happens in business that somehow stops the obvious from being done. Getting close to those involved and asking them for their input and ideas on how best to move forward with a new strategy is good practice. This builds trust, empowerment, delegation, ownership, and motivation all in one. In Sunderland in 1986 Nissan built just 5,139 cars a year, but when a senior Japanese director was walking the floor and a 25-year-old factory worker approached him with suggested changes that would improve the throughput, he listened, reflected, and they redesigned the factory to incorporate all the employee's ideas and their own views including more modern technology to now build 10,000 a week. Proper use of employee engagement!

Values

Strategy must sit alongside your business Values—and you must live these. We call it "walk the talk." The VALUES of an organization are the underlying human principles and ethics that guide the people in it. Embedded values that are sympathetic to the vision and mission can create alignment and passion within an organization that will spur people on in the pursuit of the vision. We discussed these in the brand chapter. Your values create an aspirational list of things that you expect your employees to live by. Here are some that have been used by Disney's:

Innovation: Follow a strong tradition of innovation.

Quality: Strive to follow high standards of excellence; maintain high-quality standards across all product categories.

Community: Create positive and inclusive ideas about families; provide entertainment experiences for all generations to share.

Storytelling: Every product tells a story; timeless and engaging stories delight and inspire.

Optimism: Entertainment is about hope, aspiration, and positive resolutions.

Decency: Honor and respect the trust people place in us; fun is about laughing at our experiences and ourselves.

And here some that have been used by Coca Cola:

Leadership: The courage to shape a better future

Collaboration: Leverage collective genius

Integrity: Be real

Accountability: If it is to be, it's up to me

Passion: Committed in heart and mind

Diversity: As inclusive as our brands

Quality: What we do, we do well

If you spend any time looking at company values you will see that Quality and Integrity appear a lot!

What are the values of your business? If you work for a large company, you *should* know what they are. Not only that, you *should* know what you do each day that demonstrates that value. For instance, if you have Integrity as a value in your business you should be able to say what you actually do in your job that demonstrates integrity on a daily basis. Because if you can't, then the desired values and actual values are different, and the perceived value is therefore more likely to be something totally different. Your values sit alongside your brand and, for you, as the leader of a business, alongside your personal values. If you have read the first volume of this trilogy, think back to the exercise we looked at on branding early on in that first book. Think of who you are and what you stand for. Again, if your values and the values of your business are the same, then that's a good sign. If they are polar opposites, then you'd have to question your prospects. It's not impossible for a business and the individual within it to be opposite when it comes to values, but it creates a feeling of cognitive dissonance that makes the relationship stressful, difficult, and possibly even unhealthy. The important thing about values is you must believe in them and always walk the talk, they must not be a list of words or statements that no one lives by. It is critical in attracting and keeping great employees remember that staff will be attracted to your values.

Someone looking for a new job will be focused on your values and ethics, so if you have a value which is based on commission and cash then don't be surprised to attract employees motivated by cash and bonuses. If your values are saving the world and paying back into society through corporate social responsibility programs then you can expect to attract ethical people who genuinely want to help others. So be genuine about what you want.

Imagine getting the two mixed up. These are important and must reflect your vision, mission, and brand, slogan and logo too.

In many businesses of course people are simply told what the values are, and we know that they can change overnight. But they REALLY matter and should be something very carefully worked upon. As a leader or manager you MUST walk the talk. All too often we are called to work in businesses whose espoused values include such powerful words as trust, integrity, innovation, and service, all of which are conspicuous by their absence once you actually walk in the door. It's the difference between desired and actual culture. When you last moved jobs did you spend any time looking at the business values to see if they fitted alongside your own? Think about the values in your business now. Are the stated values the same as what you experience? You must be able to live the values. And if you can't live or work by those values then either you are in the wrong business or the values need to change.

Structure

STRUCTURE is how the business is organized to achieve its strategy. Structure is a system that consists of explicit and implicit institutional rules and policies designed to outline how various work roles and responsibilities are delegated, controlled, and coordinated and determines how information flows from level to level within the company. As such it also drives culture, because it influences the way that things are done, most noticeably through imposing lines of control and authority. It is an important issue that companies have to consider. When they are in start-up mode everyone in the business does everything, but as the business grows you need individuals to be an expert in a smaller field and this also causes issues as the boss/owner becomes separated and is further away from his colleagues and the day-to-day activities. Imagine that two guys set up a business making widgets, one was a natural salesman and marketer and the other was an expert in production. They worked together in year 1. In year 2 they expanded and had 10 staff; 5 in production and 5 in sales. They still saw a lot of each other. In years 3, 4, and 5 the growth was meteoric and in year 6 they had 250 staff in 3 locations in the USA. Now they never saw each other and in the early days all the staff went out for a drink together on a Friday night. The fun had gone too as they had always enjoyed each other's company.

These businesses fail because their motivation has gone. They sold the business and never spoke to each other again.

We can all picture or recognize the business where the owner cannot let go and tries to be involved in everything and lacks trust in his baby being handled by other people. People come in, cannot work under his micro-management, and leave again. Decision making is paralyzed because nobody dares make a decision that goes against the bosses wishes. These businesses usually fail within 1 to 3 years because one person cannot do everything and knowing when to hand over is vital. I worked for a guy who knew that he was great at selling and marketing and knew he could not run a business for toffee, so as soon as he could afford it he brought in a Managing Director and said, "You run it as you see fit, I will focus on sales and marketing. All I want you to do is generate X turnover per annum, with Y profits and you will have to manage me as your sales and marketing manager too."

Other new companies focus so hard on the product they don't look at sales, marketing, collecting cash, and keeping the cash flowing—these fail too because they are internally focused on the product or service and not on the client and the cash. Culture is very important when considering the structure as it impacts greatly on the choice you make.

Let's take a look at some typical structures that we have seen. Traditional hierarchical structures are usually used by Red (direct control) and Blue (traditional, uniformed) organizations, loosely based on the military structures with a boss, directors, managers, team leaders, supervisors, and staff and power and control goes downward; if told to jump, you say "how high sir"?

Be very careful when considering structure as it really needs to line up with your culture in that if you want a very supporting culture that is helpful, engaging, and inclusive, the hierarchical structure might send out all the wrong messages. It can still be successful but watch out that the structure you choose does not conflict with your values and culture you also want.

There are advantages and disadvantages to the traditional hierarchy. Firstly, everyone knows their place and most people know what they are supposed to be doing and if someone above you tells you to do something, most staff do it without question. It is a great structure for completing tasks because it gets things done. But it is no so good at responding to problems. Organizations with hierarchical structures can be slow to adapt to change, and communication flow and information exchange is slow, and in some cases nonexistent.

Operational problems can cause a halt for traditional hierarchy organizations as the issue is referred up through the chain of command where they get discussed, and then a decision will come back down to be actioned. This structure gives management the control and there is a culture of command. The people at the bottom are least invested in and yet ironically are customer facing. Customer interactions can therefore be slow, and there is a risk that the customer experiences delays and feels ill-informed while any problems are being discussed within the business. Consequently, decisions made can feel arbitrary and lacking in personal attention.

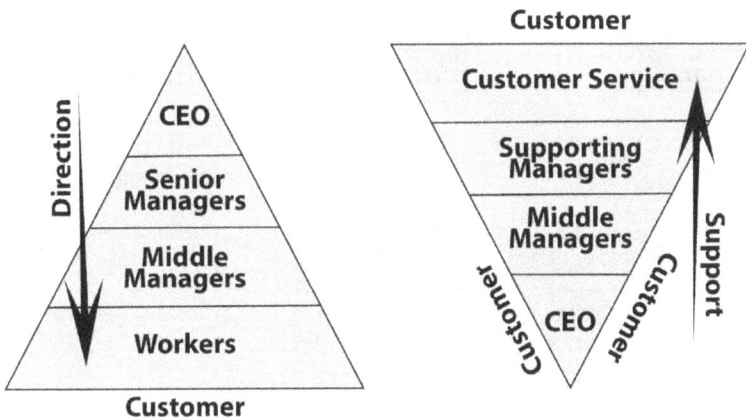

Traditional and inverted pyramid

Reverse or Inverted pyramid is more likely to be seen in green (people focused) organizations; here the focus is on other people and as such is increasingly common in businesses with a strong customer service ethic. As the name suggests, this turns the traditional hierarchy upside down, and normally emphasizes the position of the customer. Leadership styles in this business need to be different,—based more around support and service rather than dictating direction. The reverse pyramid organization places customers first, invests in customer service training for front-line staff, and is very supportive in that the managers and supervisors all support the front-line staff. Power can be difficult to use as it is an "ask" style and so power remains with employees, and it therefore can be difficult to get changes made and to discipline staff when required. One positive aspect of this structure is that customer facing staff are empowered to make decisions without needing to refer every challenge to their line manager. This can assist effective problem solving as challenges are resolved by the people closest to the customer. Consequently communication tends to feel smoother for the customer, who can feel they are being looked after more appropriately.

Strong HR is needed and managers must be well versed in the art of delegation. This is a skill many managers find hard to learn, yet in a reverse or inverted pyramid the best managers must be able to let go of their temptations to micro-manage. This allows staff free to act under their own autonomy and can be a good structure for developing trust at work.

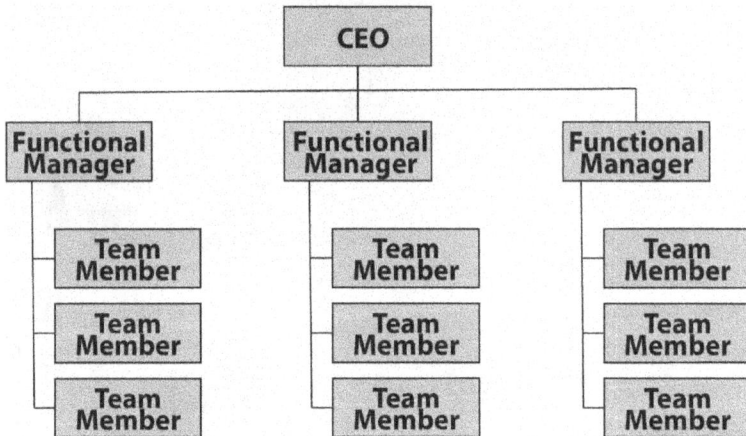

Classic functional hierarchy

Within the classical traditional hierarchy, we see teams structured by function, typically with people being organized into departments. These functional classical structures are flatter, meaning that in some businesses you can go from top to bottom of the business in just three to four steps. This keeps the business responsive and can avoid some of the paralysis that goes with deeper structures. However, as the business grows the deeper these functional structures can become, and this can make for an unwieldy and unresponsive business.

The other classic and fundamental issue we often see with this kind of structure is what we call "silo thinking." Teams work in their own way, focused on their own end-to-end process and with little consideration of, or exposure to, the challenges, aims and successes of other teams. Typically, while each team operates quite well within themselves, they experience massive problems and lack of inertia when working across teams. This is not surprising as each team is basically operating as a mini-version of the wider business, with decision making at the top level and poor customer focus. And of course in this structure other teams can be viewed as customers because they can be the consumer of the team's outputs. Expectations play a key role here as teams can build up unreasonable expectations of each other. This silo working, if unchecked and in cultures of poor communication, will typically give rise to a "them and us" feeling which can develop into a blame culture, where teams fail to meet the standards that the other teams set for them that they might not even know about. The other poor aspect of this structure is the phenomenon of "dead man's shoes", where your only chance of career advancement is if your direct line manager leaves the business. It's hard to get promotion in this structure, or to be recognized as someone who has grown and developed a role. From time to time the structure must be recast, and this normally involves much upset, significant politics, and frustration as people see sideways or downward movements in the structure as demotion.

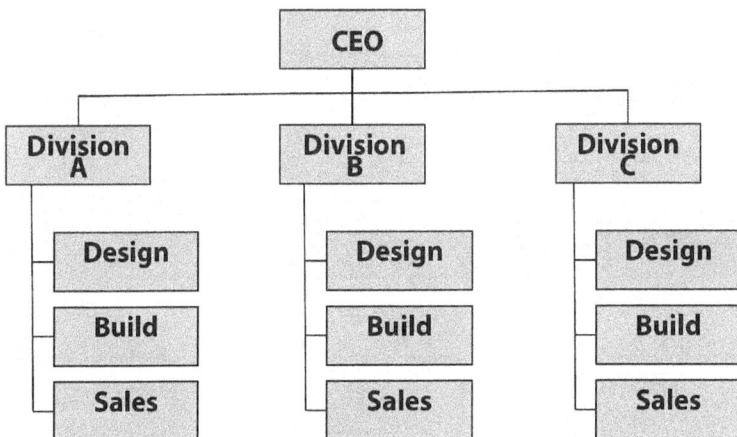

Product or divisional based hierarchy

Larger businesses often split into divisions on the argument that this allows each branch of the hierarchy to focus on its own key output. And there is some sense in this. Good examples include regional divisions of global businesses, each of which will have its own team and be fully independent of the other regions. The head office may, or may not, exercise strong control over how each division is structured. Within each division there exists a subhierarchy around stages in the process, each of which is probably structured in the classical functional way. Thus each branch of the organization might have a Sales team, and that team might be structured in a standard functional way. The risk of role duplication here can be high. Each division, for instance, might have its own Head of Finance. This can lead to politicking and wrangling across divisions, and a significant amount of parochial thinking as each Division places its own survival above the others.

One advantage of this structure is the ability to amputate one of the divisions without impacting the others, making it easy to downsize or to sell a division. While the divisional structure looks coordinated, in practice each division tends to become its own fiefdom, with cultural implications. This explains how two divisions of the same business can be so very different from one another. This makes it very hard to move jobs from one part of the business to another and makes comparison of activities extremely messy.

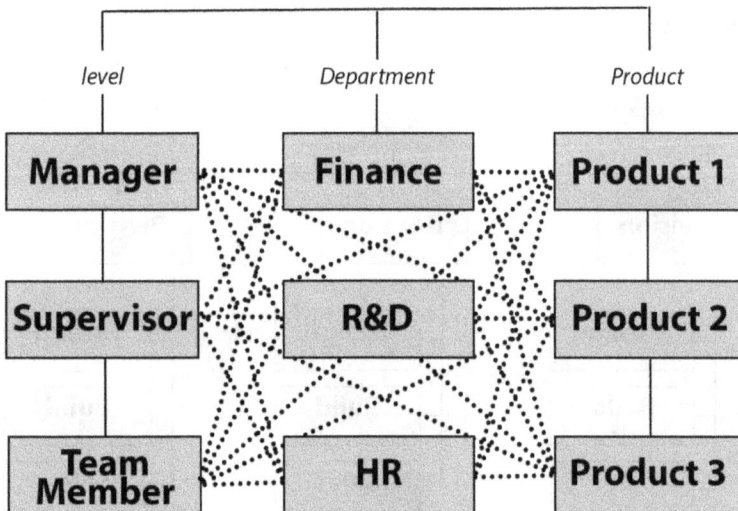

Matrix

Many modern organizations opt for a matrix organizational structure as a pragmatic line of best fit between traditional, reverse pyramid, and divisional. Matrix is a company structure in which the reporting relationships work as a grid, often with dual reporting relationships—functional and divisional. Often these structures emerge from businesses that have a divisional structure but that wish to hold certain functional standards or reporting across the business, perhaps as a response to silo working. So, a facilities management company that operates many divisions or departments with staff working on multiple projects might operate a matrix structure. Alternatively, a construction business with many sites might choose to operate a project (divisional) structure with certain core departments providing input (i.e., Finance, surveying, H&S) on a matrix basis. In this way the project or division will be responsible for organizing staff for the appropriate delivery of work with standards being set and maintained across professional functions. There are lots of positives associated with Matrix structures, but on the downside they can be difficult structures in which to work. Managers typically have to juggle many stakeholders, and active communication is essential. Once more, delegation is a crucial skill that managers need to develop if they are to develop the trust and capabilities of their team members, who must also be able to juggle conflicting priorities to respond to the ever-changing needs and requirements of other workers in the matrix.

There are other structures, but these are the ones that we see most. In truth, sometimes there is a collapsed structure, a situation in which a business is presented as one structure but operates as another. In our experience, it is not uncommon for businesses to say that they operate a matrix or reverse pyramid structure only for us to find out that the actual culture means that people experience their work as a traditional hierarchy. Typically, when these situations occur, it is through managers not feeling able to delegate and let go of power in order to allow people to be at their best. As a consequence, people feel that their autonomy is reduced and directive, top to bottom decision making steps in to fill the void.

It is well worth talking about lone workers and remote workers too where structure doesn't matter. In these structures work is done remotely and by e-mail, telephone, and the occasional face-to-face meeting. Think

Global Sales teams in Pharmaceutical companies; all working in a country where that culture has the greatest impact. Tobacco companies too have the same issues but for totally different reasons. How do you motivate, manage, and lead someone who is 5,000 miles away and can do and say what they like when they like and who they like in order to win business and sales? Yes, you can use targets and have rules and talk to them via SKYPE and internet, e-mail, mobile, landlines, web links, and conference calls but a degree of trust and freedom has to be given, and organizations who embrace these very loose structures tend to only measure results. As more and more people work from home, work when they like, maybe drive to work later in the day, go home early or, when the work is finished, require a huge degree of trust and only measuring the end results. If an employee hits all their targets every week or month and they are now on the golf course, does it matter what they are doing? Many organizations find this difficult and want to see and touch their employees, but this is changing. In 10 years' time remote and virtual teams will be prevalent. The consequences are important. Less travel to work means that fuel can be saved, pollution levels dropped, time and money saved, and a much happier workforce as they do not have to drive for 2 hours every day at 5 mph along a freeway blocked with all the other commuters all trying to arrive at 8.30 am and the same at 5.30 pm all trying to get home. With modern technology more and more time could be spent at home working or working locally in your community using shared services. Having said that we do need to interact and be with others, we are a herd animal. It is possible that all organizations could actually embrace this new way of working and perhaps the day is not far away when people drive 2 to 3 miles to a shared office to hot desk even though their employer is 50 miles away. In this Results only Work Environment[1] (ROWE), where people do not have schedules, flexible working can reach delivery real benefits of business, for individuals and for society. Work–life balance can certainly be improved, and the ability to work from home allows people with responsibilities as carers (i.e., those with responsibilities toward other family members who need particular care and support,

---

[1]An acronym first introduced and explained by Cali Ressler and Jody Thompson in 2003.

such as the elderly, very young, or infirm) to stay economically active in the work of work. Proponents of this feature argue that people can work when they want to, removing artificial blockers to productivity and engagement, and potentially delivering greater customer service in a 24/7 economy. Banks could have shared services and open one branch per high street and serve all bank customers. Dentists and doctors could open at night and weekends instead of 5 days a week, thus creating slots which suit our new needs. This could have the knock-on effect of reinvigorating high streets as community centers giving bars, cafes, and restaurants a new lease of life too. The possibilities exist. The future of work is fascinating. But we need to move on.

Tactics

Strategy, values, culture, structure, and behaviors all combine to dictate your TACTICS. Tactics are the actions you must take to deliver the strategy. This involves behavior.

In simple terms, the strategy is what I am going to try and achieve, and the tactics are the how am I going to do it? A strategy is a high-level plan to achieve one or more goals under conditions of uncertainty. Tactics are the art or science of implementing the strategy and the actions required to gain an advantage or success. This is usually achieved by having an objective; or set of objectives and overall game plan, with a set of goals and/or targets to hit or attempt to hit.

Terms such as strategy and tactics conform to the metaphor of business as a form of war. In truth, the business world is riddled with these metaphors, and many analogies can be drawn. In business we talk of strategy, tactics, campaigns, winning, attacks, divisions, companies, and even espionage; all terms that have their origins in the military world. Our military culture has become our business tradition, and our tradition in the West, and indeed in most other parts of the world, is to look at business in a similar way as one might view a grand military campaign or war.

Indulging the metaphor gives us a good way to identify the difference between strategy and tactics. Put simply, strategy is carried out by Generals, tends to plan long term, and is forward looking. Tactics are the method employed by the foot soldiers in delivering the strategy: what they do and how they do it. It tends to be doctrinal and "in the moment," with a focus on actions now as opposed to the future. Strategy and tactics can both be bloody.

For instance, the strategy of a sports team might be to win the league in 12 months' time and gain a promotion or win a cup. The tactics they will use will be to take each game at a time, favor the defense or offense, and try to win it or at least not lose it. The objectives will be to stop the other side from gaining any advantage by stopping them using their strengths or at least reducing them and exploiting their weaknesses through prior analysis and a great understanding of our strengths and playing to them so as to score one more goal than them.

Behaviors

A key aspect in the success of your tactics is behavior. It's just what you do but how you do it. BEHAVIOR is the way that values come to life within the company. Behaviors demonstrate values, they are how the values are seen in the daily behaviors of all staff, especially its leaders. This level is absolutely key, especially in organizations where customer service is a vital ingredient of success. Employees need to know how to translate values in the everyday workplace.

How SPECTRUM Behaviors Play Out in Structure and Culture

By obtaining SPECTRUM® data on a large number of people in an organization we can start to get some insight and appreciation of the way the organization, and the teams within it, might behave, and how they might appear to third parties. And knowing that can help us to reinforce and make the best of our strengths while also allowing us to identify areas for potential developments that will deliver improved organizational effectiveness.

RED   YELLOW
BLUE   GREEN

Red organizations tend to be focused on cash, profit, getting goals and targets hit, winning at all costs, and reward employees using bonuses. They control their employees using aggression. Examples would be investment banking, sales companies. Their strategies tend to be competitive, aggressive, and direct. Which is as you might expect.

Blue organizations tend to use information management, technology, rules and traditions, health and safety to manage their staff with control and a hierarchy and by the book.

Examples would be London Transport, Railways, Military.

Green organizations are focused internally on their employees and value them highly, open, discussion, coaching and asking style with no real hierarchy treating each other equally, using an ask style and leading the way by example so others will follow. Examples might be John Lewis, Netflix, Rothamsted, and Dell.

Yellow organizations are fast paced, innovative, latest technology, informal dress codes, adapting to change quickly, a bit chaotic to work for. Use fun and laughter as the model for control. Sleep pods and games to play at work, flexible working day. Examples might be SoftCat, Apple, and Google.

Lining It All Up for Strategic Direction

If you think of your business as a body, then strategic direction is the brain. It is this process that makes sense of the fact-based evidence and gut feeling intuition and tries to turn it into something concrete that can be done by people. To extend the metaphor, if strategic direction is the brain then the culture is the personality, the very thing that combines with situation to control behavior. A body that exists without a brain is trapped in a desperate physical existence where, unless supported by artificial means, the end is nigh. An active strategic process, like an active brain, can insist on changes to the physical shape of the business to keep the body healthy with the intent of giving it longevity.

We've said it before and we'll say it again. The Vision, Mission, Strategy Values, Behavior, Structure, and Tactics for your team or business MUST be aligned. Each component must support and reflect the next. We look at Desired Culture—how the top team wants to be seen by the outside world, the actual culture of how the employees treat each other, and the perceived culture which is how the customers, supply chain, and general public see the organization—it is called strategic congruence. Here is the model from the beginning again but we have now added this final bit to the jigsaw.

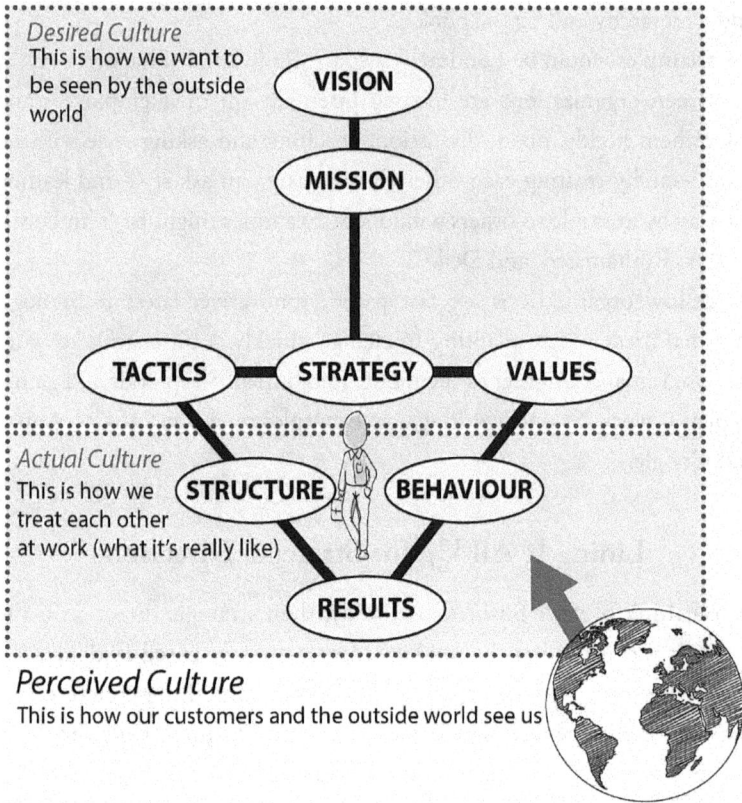

Desired Culture
This is how we want to be seen by the outside world

VISION

MISSION

TACTICS — STRATEGY — VALUES

Actual Culture
This is how we treat each other at work (what it's really like)

STRUCTURE   BEHAVIOUR

RESULTS

Perceived Culture
This is how our customers and the outside world see us

Vision, mission, strategy and culture

Have a think about alignment. Does your business or team have it? Does the behavior you see fit against the stated values? Does the strategy enable the goals? Take a look at some examples of vision statements and values that have been used by big companies and then look at your perception of them and imagine what it might be like to work for them and see if they are aligned or not.

Desired	Actual	Perceived
"We work hard every day to make American Express the world's most respected brand" (American Express)	What is it like to work for Amex?	What do you think about Amex?
"It is our goal to be earth's most customer-centric company, where customers can find and discover anything they might want to buy online" (Amazon)	What do the employees say about Amazon?	What do you think about Amazon as a customer? 1 in 3 use them in the UK
"To be the ultimate house of luxury, defining style and creating desire, now and forever!" (Chanel)	Are the staff in tune with this?	It is certainly a leading top-end brand and it is expensive, exclusive, and considered a luxury
"To refresh the world in mind, body and spirit. To inspire moments of optimism and happiness through our brands and actions. To create value and make a difference" (Coca Cola)	Do the staff agree?	Do you agree too?
"To give people the power to share and make the world more open and connected" (Facebook)	Employees view of Facebook?	Your opinion of Facebook?
"To organise the world's information and make it universally accessible and useful." (Google)	What is it like to work for Google?	What do all the home and business users think about the world's biggest search engine and information provider?
"To bring inspiration and innovation to every athlete in the world — if you have a body you are an athlete!" (Nike)	Nike employees feel free to comment here?	Have you got any Nike products? What do you think of them?

Remember these Golden Rules about Strategic Direction

Your business (and your team) needs VISION, a MISSION, STRUC-TURE, CULTURE, STRATEGY, VALUES, and then GOALS, which must be in alignment if you want total success. All of these concepts feed into and influence each other.

Your VALUES are important in helping to shape the way that you deliver those goals. Those values need to be consistent with your BRAND and with your own behaviors.

If your values and the values of the business are at odds, one of you needs to change—or get out.

STRUCTURE matters. In general, you can have control or customer centricity. Businesses, of course, strive for both and so structures are often a messy compromise. Yet a clear structure will provide a strong skeleton around which your people will perform great things.

STRUCTURE and TACTICS influence what people do and how they do it. They dictate how you control and focus your business. Let go of as much as you can and resist the temptation to micro-manage.

CHAPTER 2

W Is for "What If . . . ?"

Do You Know What to Do in Those "What If . . ." Moments?

"Every time I think 'What if I am wrong?' There is another whisper deep inside which says What if I am right?"

—Sanji Paul Arvind

In business you will be faced with a huge number of "what ifs." What would the result be if an action does, or doesn't work? What if we do the wrong thing? What if the market shifts? What if we train our staff and they leave? What if we don't train them and they stay?

In this chapter we talk about the power of what ifs from three prime perspectives. Firstly the power of visualization to allow you to be prepared for the what if as it happens on an individual level. Then we talk about how you can prepare your team to perform in a world that is volatile, uncertain, complex, and ambiguous, and finally we talk about how we use the spectrum model to help us understand how our behavioral preferences influence the way we regard "what if" scenarios.

The smart leader thinks ahead.

What If . . . . the Power of Visualization

Sports coaches have known for some time that visualization techniques work. They use this approach for golfers, cricketers, NFL kickers, tennis players, boxers, weightlifters, athletes, rowers, skiers, gymnasts, racing drivers, jockeys, baseball players, basketball players, and just about any other sportsperson you can think of.

Visualization is the technique of being able to see, in your mind's eye, a situation and the actions you will take to perform the right hit, kick, punch, swing, throw, volley, or act that delivers a perfect outcome. In its simplest form, it is a method of mental rehearsal for an act that you will need to perform in the future. Visualization gives you a chance to run through the event in your mind and respond to what you see in that vision. It is a chance to prepare to be great, but also a chance to prepare for those "what if" moments.

We all look back on things and wonder what we might have done differently. Sometimes we look back and wish that we had acted in a way that was different to the way we actually behaved or acted. That is called "regret." Nobody likes a life filled with regrets. As Sinatra once sang; "Regrets? I've had few, but then again, too few to mention."[1]

The actor Jim Carrey claimed that he visualized for many years what it would be to be a Hollywood superstar. The great Mohammed Ali was also an advocate of visualization. Surely everyone wants to dream of being the best that they can be in their chosen field? But visualizations are not simply dreams. They are more controlled and focused than dreams. The thing with dreams is they are too dreamy. A visualization takes you to another level. A visualization transports you completely to the moment, so you experience the moment as if for real. It is a spiritual, mental, and physical focus that leaves you with a template in your mind that you can use in the real event. The act of visualization prepares our mind to be sharp in the moment, so that when we see an event or situation unfolding in the present, we can apply the wisdom of our previous visualization and know what to do for the best. Some might say this is called intuition, but while intuition might shape our behavior, visualization is not the same thing as intuition.

There is a body of research that reveals that thoughts produce the same mental instructions as actions, highlighting the strength of the mind–body connection and the link between thoughts and behaviors.

---

[1]From the classic song, "My Way"; written by Paul Anka

There are a few things that we suggest you do to improve the impact of your visualization practice and improve your chances of success.

When you visualize a situation, do so from as many different angles as possible. So when you are visualizing the perfect pitch or presentation think; do not just think about what it takes to deliver the presentation, running through again and again in your mind from a number of different perspectives. Try it from the perspective of a member of the audience or your presentation skills coach. What will onlooker see as they peer through the window? This gives you a chance to identify and connect not only to what is going on for you, but also what is going on for others.

Secondly, these visualizations need to be made using all of your senses. What will it *feel* like to give that drop dead perfect speech? What will you *see*? What will you *hear* and *smell*?

What will you *touch*? How will you be *standing*? What will your voice *sound* like (don't hang up too much on the words themselves). What will the *taste* be like in your mouth? Will you feel hot? Cold? Cool? What will your audience be seeing? What will they be *hearing*? How will they *feel*? What will they be *saying*? What about the voice coach? How will she be *feeling*? Will she feel proud, be smiling, maybe doing a fist pump! The more you can visualize and experience these things mentally in your mind's eye the greater the likelihood of you having a great outcome when you do the thing for real.

Once you have visualized, you should continue your life as if you have already nailed that goal. So when you come back from the visualization of the person who has just delivered the best speech of their career, retain the feeling of success and positivity that goes with that. If you can go into that situation with the positive feelings of success already in your mind and heart then you are far more likely to pull off a fantastic outcome than if you go on stage with all the self-doubt, fear, and nerves of a stage-struck idiot. Choose the way you want to feel.

To this end we support the idea of positive self-talk and surrounding yourself with reminders of what success looks like for you. Again, we can take a lead from sports coaches here. I once worked with a performance coach who had coached national teams to success. He felt that one of the simplest and most effective tools that he ever used was to ask each player to talk to him about their crowning career moment so far. He asked them to bring a photo of that successful moment and to sit with him and talk that moment through with him, to explain what it felt like to be a winner. He then had the facilities team put that picture above the player's hook in the changing room so that they would have a simple reminder of what it felt like to be at their best, and knowing that seeing that image would raise the same emotions in them and spur them to success.

There is a well-known phrase that we use a lot with clients. You probably know it: "Whether you think you can or think you can't, you're right." Positive self-talk can create confidence and grow your self-belief and can influence your ability to do the right thing at the right time. This positivity can make you seize the initiative when you are faced with that "what if" moment and step you toward a positive and best outcome and steer you away from regret.

Businesses can also visualize, although the processes are slightly different, as we shall now reveal.

Time Travel for Teams

One excellent way to try this out for yourself is to take your team on a time travel journey. In this exercise you propel yourself forward in time to a point in the future. This may be 1 year, 3 years, 5 years, or more. What will the world be like then? What would your business need to be doing to satisfy the needs of the market?

My dear old dad once gave me a desktop calendar. It was one of those desktop ones on which every date there is a new "thought for the day." I'm not really sure of the theme, dad had used a few days of it himself, so the cover was long gone. He gave it to me when I was at his house and he was clearing his desk. He knew I loved these life quote things, so he threw it at me and said, "there you go." In general, I suppose the quotes, most of which are attributed to "great thinkers" throughout history, would be considered as "life tips." Not my dear old dad's cup of tea at all, hence the handover. He knows me well.

I remember the day. It was the 12th April. The top quote read: "We never do anything well until we cease to think about the manner of doing it" and is attributed to William Hazlitt. I'd never heard of Hazlitt so I googled him to assess his credentials for such a statement (a nice piece of blue behavior by me). A contemporary of William Wordsworth and Samuel Coleridge, Hazlitt was a philosopher, journalist, and essayist in early 19th-century Britain. According to The Hazlitt Society he became the first major drama critic in English, the first major art critic, and one of the most gifted literary and general essayists in English. Considered a lifelong radical, he was one of those men whose ideas and challenges helped drive cultural and intellectual development in the early years of the industrial revolution. And I'd never heard of him.

Part of me agrees with Hazlitt. Think for a moment about top sportsmen who develop fantastic muscle memory to be at the top of their game. This success comes through practice, natural skill, a reading of the game, and, as we have seen, a lot of visualization. It's smooth and well-practiced and definitely efficient. But does Hazlitt's quote have validity in the workplace?

We often like to think of our organizations as efficient machines where activities become smooth, well-practiced, and consistent with Hazlitt's view. But there is a danger in that. If, to quote Hazlitt, we "cease to think about the manner of doing," then over time smooth and well-practiced becomes faded and outdated. The outside world moves on while the organization stands still. And that's bad. To cease thinking about the way we do things is to overlook possible areas of development. If we all accepted the status quo and ceased thinking about the manner of doing, then where would creative new ideas come from? If we want to develop then we must constantly challenge the way that we do things. We need to ask more "what if . . ." questions.

One of the questions that I ask people to consider is why do you do what you do? If they can answer that then the follow-up is why do you do it in the way that you do? This is sometimes more difficult to answer, requiring them to reevaluate the purpose of the activity and the possible alternative methods. It can also help to draw out some underlying values and beliefs that shape (and sometimes constrain) our view of the world. In other words, making ourselves stop and consider the answer to these questions allows us to apply creative thinking in the workplace—to allow more time for "what if . . . ." And that's got to be a good thing, hasn't it?

Using "What If . . . ." to Build Resilience

Think of a successful organization as a healthy athlete. Honed, toned, in the zone and eager for success. Reaching the pinnacle of Olympic success takes time, commitment, vision, and only comes with dedicated practice and preparation. This preparation comes in different forms—mental and physical—and all with the aim of being at your best when the moment of truth arrives. As already mentioned, coaches ask their athletes to visualize what it will feel like to compete and to imagine in great detail how they will feel in those vital moments when there is all to gain, or all to lose. What does success look like? What will it take to win through? How will it feel to do so? What needs to happen for success to be realized?

The same preparatory techniques can be applied to organizations, where simulations can form part of this preparation, helping the organization develop and maintain its vision during periods of stress in a way that allows it to preserve competitive edge, standing at the top of its game, honing and toning and making it alert to critical moments and allowing it to be the first to act when the need arises (making fast decisions using the OODA[2] loop). But by thinking ahead and asking some important "what if" questions such critical moments might be avoidable. In short, preparing your teams through "what if" planning makes your business more resilient.

Look at these two definitions of resilience:

The essence of resilience is therefore the intrinsic ability of an organisation to maintain or regain a dynamically stable state which allows it to continue operations after a major mishap and/or in the presence of continuous stress. (Weick and Sutcliffe 2001)

[Resilience is] . . . the capacity of a system, enterprise, or a person to maintain its core purpose and integrity in the face of dramatically changed circumstances. (Zolli 2012)

---

[2]The OODA loop is a decision-making loop based around Observe, Orient, Decide, and Act. It is attributed to United States Air Force Colonel John Boyd, who used it to understand how US fighter pilots were able to beat high-quality Chinese MIG fighters during the Korean War.

Good decision-making exercises, business simulations, and war games can help organizations develop this resilience.

We know that key predictors of continuity effectiveness and organizational resilience in critical situations include managerial style, leadership attitudes, delegation culture, reporting structures, and decision-making procedures. We also know that diversity and the workings of the informal system are crucial factors in the way that organizations embed resilience.

Simulations can be an essential tool in the identification and development of these attributes, understanding how they may influence, benefit, or possibly at times hinder our quest for excellence.

Put your hand in the air if you would be happy to climb onboard an aircraft with a pilot who had not been trained in dealing with an emergency? I can't see you, but the chances are that your hand is still firmly down by your side. Most of us wouldn't dream of such a situation. In the airline industry the impact of unexpected events can quite literally have tragic consequences. We expect that pilots are trained to know how to react in critical situations. For organizations operating in other sectors the impacts of critical incidents may not directly impact life or death but can create enough excessive pressure to flip the organization into or toward chaos. A good and well-trained pilot has a chance of regaining control, whereas an ill-prepared or poorly trained pilot may not. I know which I would rather fly with.

There is a difference of course between planned and unplanned events. Systems (and organizations exist as systems don't forget) are generally good at dealing with anticipated critical events but are extremely fragile when unanticipated events rise up to create stress and threaten the stable state. When these events occur, the organization will look to its managers and its leaders to respond. Time to step up to the plate and be counted. Useful then if you have some experience of what to expect.

Developing managers and leaders to cope with such critical situations is not easy, not least because the range of potential situations is so vast. Sit down with a pen and a vivid imagination and very soon you'll have a disaster movie in the making. But think about your own career and the challenging moments you have faced, and you begin to imagine how even the most every day scenarios can generate extraordinary experiences. Some potential critical scenarios may seem fantastic, and skeptics will often counter the idea of potential scenarios with cries of "That'll never happen," but the fact is these incidents do occur. Organizations are frequently responding to unforeseen events. Just pick up a newspaper or flick to your favorite online news source to realize that these events are all around us, all the time.

And they are not restricted to large organizations. Smaller enterprises may face equally tough times, arguably with greater potential for long-term impact. These events could be enormous, catastrophic, and tragic (such as a terrorist strike) or deeply problematic (such as the loss of a key employee or major contract). Although these events may seem very distant from each other, each creates stress on the fabric of the organization, and leaders need to step up and take action. We have to equip our organizations to cope with the uncertainty that such events create, and that means preparing managers and leaders to think flexibly, responsibly, and appropriately in difficult situations. Critical events do not develop in a linear fashion—that's inherent in their very nature. They are surrounded by "friction," those unanticipated but all too real forces that create additional uncertainty. These can feed a positive feedback loop, where events can spiral, and the situation can become very unstable, very quickly. When they do, nonresilient organizations will be ill prepared and will find it much harder to bounce back. Resilience in organizations occurs when the system continues to operate despite failures in some of its parts and despite the disturbances caused by critical events. It means navigating some stormy waters in perilous winds, and the maelstrom can be destructive.

But there is also an amazingly constructive side to these incidents. Real critical incidents and good simulations create environments conducive to innovation. They provide excellent learning opportunities and generate new thinking. By using simulations, business war games, and red team exercises, organizations can reap the positives of learning without being threatened by the negatives.

Using Creative Exercises to Explore "What If"

Such exercises use real-world scenarios to engage and develop leaders. They allow leaders to assess the strategic and operational readiness of their business. Most importantly, they challenge existing thinking and provide leadership teams with a credible exercise that tests decision making, exposes weak spots, spotlights talent, and creates real space for quality and operationally specific learning.

Run as a facilitated event over a series of phases, simulation exercises and workshops are our TARDIS[3] to the future, creating a time traveling vehicle that enables our exploration to begin.

These interactive people-based decision-making exercises can create an escalating set of conditions that allows a team of participants to move their thinking ahead of the present day and forward to the point where they are experiencing the future. Over the past we have used these with considerable success, heading off anything from ethical protests to sales slumps.

And this can all be done without leaving your boardroom, and without using up terabytes of computer data. It need not involve techies, geeks, or weirdoes (although you are free to provide your own!). Instead, simulations focus on the human side of the change experience, allowing the managers and leaders in your organization to face and experience the challenges of the future in a risk free present-day setting. Creating scenarios that move your business into the future moves us into the complex domain, where conditions of uncertainty make decision making difficult. Simulations are a place for experiential and pragmatic learning.

They allow you to explore the "what if . . ." and move teams to a place where an escalating situation delivers new challenges and can allow the team to change their thinking and to create vision of the future that might otherwise have been out of reach.

As the Time Traveler in HG Wells' story puts it, "Scientific people know well that time is only a kind of space." By taking our simulation forward in time we can create the space to do great work today. When the exercise is complete, delegates return to the current and share their experiences and insights. What is the future like? What attributes, characteristics, behaviors, and systems will the future require? What new talents and capabilities are needed? What disasters can be prevented? What actions can we take now to create the best future? Who are the best people to get us there?

As we analyze these learnings it becomes easier to visualize just what the future might look like. It becomes possible to understand more about

---

[3]A time travelling vehicle used by the TV character Dr Who

the relationship between cause and effect and it allows the first steps to be taken in a change process to move closer toward a future that can now be visualized and communicated. The exercise allows you the creative space needed to assess future strategies and aims.

These exercises go by different names. At one end of the scale are continuity exercises, shifting your organization through time to a critical moment where rapid and often stress-filled decisions are the order of the day. At the other might be multiteam large-scale military, political, or business war games, where hundreds of agents and systems play out an interconnected and shared future. In between are the leadership, strategic change, and corporate visioning decision-making exercises where management teams take their time machine to a new space in the quest of future proofing and resilience. At the very entry level is a focus on your project, your team, your individual situation.

Creative exercises are a hotbed for talent development. When exercises like these are held you can actually see the process of team formation, alignment, and power politics being played out before your very eyes. Team members who might previously have seemed the most unlikely achievers can step up and unveil talents that were previously not noticed. On the other hand, others might face a struggle coming to terms with the emerging fact that their long-held beliefs and strategies are not future proof.

Business war games work on a team basis, with one team (drawn from your managers) taking on the role of your competitors or other challengers intent on creating a strategy that endangers your core business. The second team acts as your management team, creating strategy and proactively countering the other team in an attempt to stay ahead. What follows serves to challenge existing thinking, encourages innovation, tests leadership, promotes team working, and allows the best members of your team to step up and be counted.

The quality of these exercises comes in the scoping and understanding of the starting point of the present day and to understand about the outcomes that you want to get from the exercise. And a growth mindset. As to the exercise itself, they range in time from anything from half a day to half a week, with teams working independently or in a multigroup system (some of the best exercises involve teams working in competition with each other, making move and countermove in a style faithful to your industry).

In summary, these approaches allow a full exploration of the "what if . . ." questions surrounding your business and are also great for the following:

| STIMULATE | SPOTLIGHT | PROMOTE | IDENTIFY |
| Creativity | Talent | Resilience | Blindspots |

8 KEY BENEFITS OF SIMULATIONS AND DECISION MAKING EXERCISES

www.poppyfish.co.uk

| CHALLENGE | ENCOURAGE | DEVELOP | MAXIMISE |
| Existing thinking | Teamwork | Leaders | Return on budget |

1. Stimulating innovative and creative thinking in a low-risk environment

   A realistic scenario allows learners to experience the type of decision-making challenge that they will only face in moments of crisis—moments that they do not come across in their day-to-day working lives. Such activities provide opportunities to stimulate innovative and creative thinking in a low-risk environment. The process of being involved in a closed door session serves to focus the mind of managers and leaders on the scenario and allows focused discussion in a way that the normal day-to-day activities do not allow.

2. Challenging standard paradigms and strategic thinking

   Decision-making exercises, red teams, simulations, and business war games create the types of situational thinking and awareness that generates new thinking, sometimes in some areas very fundamental to the business, its aims, and its strategy. Such events can be a great way of assessing the suitability of selected strategies. In this way, they challenge standard mental paradigms and strategic thinking.

3. Identifying blind spots and new opportunities

   As Weick and Sutcliffe (2001) tell us, "In that brief interval between surprise and successful normalizing lies one of your few opportunities to discover what you don't know." There are few better ways to assess the viability of a new strategy, campaign, or initiative than to pit the concept through a red team, simulation, or business war game. These events can help to identify blind spots in your thinking or levels of preparation that, when actively assessed, can improve resilience and stimulate innovative solutions.

4. Spotlighting talent

   Participating in such events can see unsung heroes emerge from within your team. There is a saying that when the going gets tough, the tough get going. But we often don't know how people will fare in uncertain situations. Decision-making exercises, red teams, simulations, and business war games can allow you to see how your team works together in conditions of uncertainty and can provide a platform allowing you to spotlight talent in your team. They can help you identify individuals who have the talent to succeed and to observe them in interaction with their peers outside of their normal operating environment. If fed back appropriately, these learnings can be useful in developing the emotional intelligence of those involved.

5. Developing foresight

   Having foresight means that leaders and managers are equipped to think ahead of the game and be prepared and adaptable enough to cope with emerging and complex scenarios.

   Simulations, by their very nature, can help to promote resilience at the individual and the team level, preparing people for a real situation that they may face in their workplace. As such these events promote resilience by allowing individuals to feel prepared for the situation they may face.

6. Encouraging teamwork and collaboration

   Decision-making exercises, red teams, simulations, and business war games encourage team working and collaboration. In the simulation as in the real world, cooperation and team work are important components of success. Such events provide a forum for building team relationships and highlights dependencies between groups. Simulations allow the stresses and strains between groups to be identified, explored, and improved, providing greater assurance that they will work more effectively when the need comes.

7. Promoting resilience at the individual and the team level

Organizations exist as complex systems of teams and individuals and knowing how those teams might act in a certain situation is valuable data. Building resilience at the individual and team level promotes the resilience of the wider organization. Individuals taking part in red teams, simulations, decision-making exercises, and business war games all have an opportunity to develop their self-awareness and emotional intelligence, which can help to improve resilience and mindfulness. Thus, such events can serve as effective individual development skills for leaders and managers, allowing them to develop skills and competencies that are useful not only in their current roles but that might also be portable to other roles and which will undoubtedly strengthen their overall portfolio.

8. Maximizing return on L&D spending

The final point is financial. Budgets are pressured. Bespoke decision-making exercises, war games, and simulations maximize the return on learning and development spending. Participants in such events typically speak of the quality of the learning being generated as being far superior to any standard training course or event. In addition, the individuals and teams involved spend the entire time in the exercise thinking about your own organization and the real challenges that they face and learn how to work with each other in the process. Participants leverage learning in a multidisciplinary environment working alongside colleagues in a realistic way. Few other learning opportunities provide such interactive and workplace-specific learning.

And the other thing about such sessions is that they combine hard thinking, strong learning, and critical evaluation with fun, camaraderie, and a sense of purpose. And who wouldn't want that?

The SPECTRUM Model and "What If . . ." Scenarios

Individual responses to what if . . . scenarios and situations have a connection to our appetite for risk. When faced with a what if then my behavior preferences will influence the way I am likely to respond.

What If . . . . for Reds

For people with a red preference what if is more than just a dilemma, it's a challenge. A throwing down of a gauntlet that is as tantamount to saying, "go on then, do this." With a proclivity toward action people with a red preference have a lower fear of risk and are more likely to act first and think later. However, if all does not go according to plan they will have no regrets and will quickly move on to the next thing. Reds do not dwell on the past, they move on very quickly. So, when faced with a "what if" scenario at work the red person is likely to say "let's go for it," with an emphasis on getting it done quickly. Red is much more likely to focus on the potential gains to be had from the new direction and will not be so bothered about losses. This may be great, and there are surely times when this approach works and gets great outcomes, but there is a risk that corners get cut along the way. The red person needs to be aware of their predisposition toward action, and may need to consciously think and ask more questions before the leap in.

What If . . . . for Blues

Mr Red's blue counterpart is much more risk conscious and is much more likely to focus on what might be lost by taking the new direction. The blue decision-making process is slower and more deliberate; "Measure twice and cut once" is their philosophy. There may be lots of reasons why the "what if" spells danger, and if you want to know what these are then ask a blue person. When blues are involved in any decision-making process it will be thorough, but it will be slow. They want all the information there is to know before they can make a decision. If they could, they would remove the "if" altogether from the equation so there is no ambiguity. The trouble often is that you'd not have the time. "What ifs" are sometimes spur of the moment, and Mr Blue is not a spur of the moment kind of guy. Hence, he might let opportunities pass him by, and, unlike Mr Red, blue preferenced people will have regret, and the irony is that this experience will probably make them want to go even slower next time (and be even more blue) so they don't make the same mistake again.

So, when faced with a "what if" our blue people must be prepared to go ahead without perfect knowledge and, at times, act without knowing what the outcome will be. This will create stress for them, which they will remain tightlipped about.

What If . . . . for Yellows

People with a yellow behavioral preference love a what if. They thrive on the chance to create something new and so are always attracted to a different or new direction. Like reds, they will have no regrets if it goes wrong, and will not accept responsibility for the error, believing instead that "we" made the mistake and that it was "our" decision. This lack of ownership gives them a great defense against regret, of which they genuinely have none. The yellow can also be highly persuasive toward others, with a natural focus on the positives that might arise from the new direction. They are a natural go-for-it person. Because they can jump straight in with both feet they can be seen as poor decision makers, especially by blues. Yellows are not detailed focused, which of course frustrates blue massively, but the yellow manager or leader who wants to make fewer poor decisions when faced with "what if" scenarios might do well to give some airtime to his or her blue companions, who can apply some history, process, and logic to the challenge.

What If . . . . for Greens

Greens are the great consultors and questioners, always asking others if they are OK. Thus, they may overlook their own natural instincts at times when faced with a "what if" and take a route that they think makes other people happy. If they get it wrong they will have regrets, and they will blame themselves for the whole thing, and maybe get very emotional about it. Greens do have massive empathy though, so hearing their opinions on how they see a situation can be insightful—especially if you ask them to do it as if they were in someone else's shoes. They are really good at this.

Greens desire perfection, so they will always have a tendency to steer away from "what ifs" that just don't quite give them the perfect outcome, and, like blue, they might feel swamped with the pressure of having to make a decision faced with lots of possible outcomes. The great strength of green though is their collaborative skills, being able to work well with others to encourage them to bring their strengths to the table. They therefore have an important role to play regarding inclusivity in teams and taking a facilitative approach to "what if" scenarios.

Remember These Golden Rules for What If . . . Situations

Visualization techniques can prepare you to be at your best. Scenario exercises develop people and build resilience.

Critical incidents can take many forms. What critical incidents are likely to affect your team? What will the impact be? How probable is it that they will occur. Remember that this is more than risk management; this is about training your people in such a way that they have a framework for decision making in times of criticality.

It is generally better to do something than do nothing. Design scenarios to test your team. Use decision-making exercises, continuity exercises, and even business wargames to help you. Watch how people react. What can they learn? How can you help them?

People have different attitudes to risk. Use Spectrum to get the right balance. It's OK to get it wrong. Just don't do it twice.

CHAPTER 3

E Is for Evidence

Can You Find the Evidence to Back Your Intuition?

"Tell people there's an invisible man in the sky who created the universe, and the vast majority will believe you. Tell them the paint is wet, and they have to touch it to be sure."

—George Carlin

Evidence is defined as the available body of facts or information indicating whether a belief or proposition is true or valid. In our sense we are interested in the evidence to back your hunches and minimize the threat of risk. There will be times in your business life when you will need to gain information to support an initiative, to discover more about a question or an issue, maybe even just to prove to yourself that others see things in the same way as you. In this chapter we will look at how to gather "facts," how to capture the opinions and thoughts of others, and how to ask great questions. The combination of all of these skills and approaches should enable you to confidently gather the evidence you need for whatever case you are attempting to build.

Why Do We Even Need Evidence?

Evidence gives us the confidence to act on a firm basis of fact. It gives us a certainty from which we can make clear interpretations. As we have already seen, in business we always want to have the best information available so that we can make the best decisions.

These truths can be harder to see as we look out through our organization and into other teams, divisions, companies, markets, and even globally into different cultures.

Things that are close to us are easy to see (they are more based in fact), but when things are further removed from us, the more uncertain they become and the harder it is for us to trust what is happening. And what happens in the absence of facts is that we will make up our own opinions formed from our own bias and previous experience. The fewer points of fact that we can identify, the more this fantasy plays out. This model of fact, faction, fiction, and fantasy is a central concept of Mick Cope in his excellent book "The Seven Cs of Coaching: A Definitive Guide to the Collaborative Coaching," in which he uses his "Fantasy Ladder" to help coaches allow people to reflect and review on the world around them. Let's explore and apply this in more detail. You know what you do in your job. No one sees it or knows it like you do, it's your world, and you live it every day. This is reality, or, in other words, this is FACT. But let's move away from you one step and look at your boss's world. You have a good idea of what your boss does, after all, you see a lot of it, but you see it through a lens;—your lens; so what you see is just a particular angle. What you see of his or her job is not fact, but a biased[1] view from your perspective, which can be called FACTION.

Now then, what about your boss's boss? This person is a further step away from you in the hierarchy so you know even less about them. You probably have a vague idea of how he or she spends his or her time but they are too distant to see clearly. You hear stories and you see stuff, again filling in the gaps with stories that you make up based on those facts as you see them. This is similar to the faction view of the world of your boss, but as your boss's boss is even further away from you then you tend to make up even more of your own stories to fill the gaps. There is less fact, and more making it up. So, let's call that FICTION. You have a fictional view of that world and can only guess much of what happens. And finally, what about your boss's-boss's-boss, someone three places above you in the work hierarchy? Well, they might as well be on the moon. The chances

---

[1]Of course, strictly speaking, your own view of your own world could be bias, but let's not go there today!

are that you know virtually nothing about this person's job other than the title and one or two things that you might come into direct contact with. How does he or she really spend their day? You have no idea, but you can imagine and, as before you make up the gaps, but this time there are so many of them that the factual content almost disappears. So, let's call this imagination as FANTASY and we'll be close to the truth. So, in terms of our organizational and individual knowledge or view of what is going on at work, it goes from FACT, to FACTION, to FICTION, to FANTASY.

Now look sideways through teams and you can see this even more clearly. I know what my team does. They're great, getting through as much as they do under all kinds of pressures and with all that domestic baggage, and with a terrible IT system too. Yeah, we're great. Now look sideways into the next team. Well, they're ok, they don't give us the time we need though, they seem pretty self-obsessed. Frank is OK and Delia is a star. Just make sure you avoid Franco. And what about the team beyond them? Well, they have to work with Desmond, he's a control freak so their life must be hell. They always look so miserable and I saw one of them in tears last week. And what about the team the other side of them? Well, they're never in the office, so they can't do much. Most of them look like dropouts.

I'm sure you can relate to this. So, if you were asked to lead a business improvement initiative you can see that while you may be working with facts for your own team, you don't have to go very far away to have an idea of what is happening and we make things up. But you might say "A-ha" that doesn't apply to me because I know everybody in all teams person- ally and have great in-depth knowledge of what's happening. That might be true, but there will still be areas where this applies. Perhaps think of your neighbors. If you live on a regular street with neighbors either side then this plays out too. You know your own house and the people in it, and you know exactly what happens when the curtains are closed. You know your immediate neighbors who live next door well enough to have a pretty good idea of what's going on there, and the people the other side of them? Well, you borrowed his lawn mower once so he seems a nice guy and his wife (are they married?) always waves hello and drives a nice car so she must have a pretty good job. And what about the people next to them? Comings and goings all through the night, police cars outside, and the garden all overgrown and drainpipes almost hanging off. They must be drug dealers!

Of course on weighing up the evidence there are a million possible explanations for what you see but without evidence you just make it up. Maybe the people in the far house are police officers, working long hours on night shift and calling in from time to time while on their shift. And maybe they rent the house and are in legal dispute with the landlord over the upkeep. Who knows which is right? It's just your fantasy.

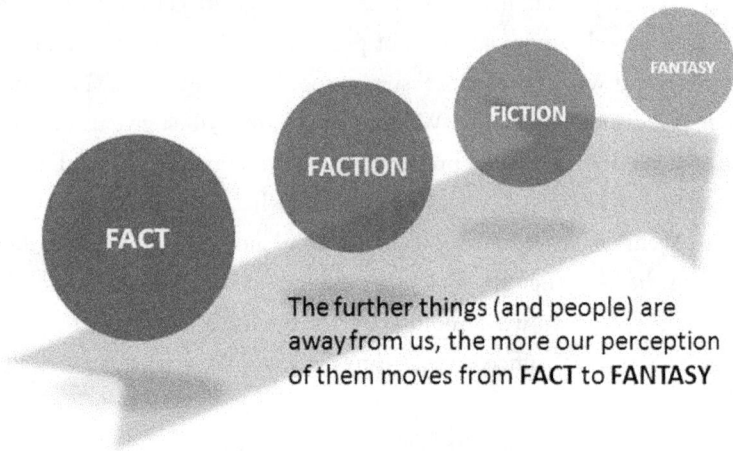

The further things (and people) are away from us, the more our perception of them moves from **FACT** to **FANTASY**

If we make decisions based on fantasy then we risk making some really bad choices. In the work example, if the manager were to act on his current base of knowledge he would only see less than 25 percent of the real situation as affecting all teams, and yet we know that in businesses people do make decisions based on this situation. To be fair to everyone and to get the best outcome for all we need to be collecting information and evidence.

The first thing to remember about gathering of evidence is that it is not the same as gathering of information. Information is knowledge without purpose, whereas evidence is specific, relevant information that is pertinent to the situation I am seeking to understand. What you need when making persuasive business pitches and presentations is powerful and targeted information.

Background Commercial Market and Business Data

Hooray for the Internet! The massive growth in the availability of information from online sources in the past twenty years has been phenomenal. Just type what you want to know into Google and within 10 minutes you can compile a whole load of data. Some of it might be good quality, and some of it might be, as President Trump might say, "Fake News." You need to be able to distinguish between good-quality data and a biased view.

I'm going to make a huge assumption here, which is that you'd rather see good quality and reliable data and information and not the biased or ill-researched view. I say assumption, because we all know that there might be times when you want to use particular data and facts to give a sway to the case. But let's stick to quality information for now.

If you are putting together a business plan or case to senior management then it's quite likely that you'll be looking to find market data. Market research companies will very happily sell you their latest marketing report on a product, business, or industry but you can expect to pay a high price for it. Most large companies publish an annual report detailing their views on the market and giving financial data, which can normally be accessed free of charge from their websites. National governments also offer information on companies, with certain information being available to download (for instance in the UK from Companies House).

Credit checks are also available through a number of online agencies from which you will receive a snapshot of the financial health of the business you are researching. These credit reports are worth investing in if you plan to extend credit to a customer, and can indicate to you (although not always with 100 percent accuracy) whether the business is in a strong financial condition.

Testing Your Intuition

As a manager within a business though, most of the time you'll be faced with making decisions that have a larger internal than external significance: changing software systems, processes, and procedures to make the business more efficient. In this case we would recommend one simple fact-finding methodology: Reduce the amount of fantasy in your current mindset by seeking input and information from as many people as you possibly can, and if you are tasked with making changes to solve what others see as a problem, ask those other people about how they see the problem and what they would do about it.

This can be done in any number of ways: but the ones we like best of all are

A) Focus groups and facilitated workshops
B) Diagonal interviews
C) Shadowing
D) Customer feedback and NPS
E) Back to the floor

Focus Groups and Facilitated Workshops

Focus groups and facilitated workshops bring people together to explore a topic. These workshops form a core part of our organizational development work and they ALWAYS generate huge amounts of data and stimulate high energy and engagement around the topic. In a focus group or facilitated workshop we bring a number of invited people together and ask them to work together to explore an idea, issue, or problem. This is normally structured so the groups work through a planned day of exercises designed to firstly take the lid off an issue and then explore it. We follow the model of facilitation shown in the diagram, firstly to explore gently and then to delve deeply into a topic before tying the loose ends back together at the end. The environment for these sessions must be informal, comfortable, and have plenty of space. When we run these workshops we use Neuland Pinpoint Facilitation boards, six-foot-tall pin boards that allow people to get creative. But you can work with whiteboards, post-its, or just about any other method you choose. The session should be run by someone who has a good moderation/facilitation style and probably should not be someone too close to the issue. Our advice is take a whole day, do it somewhere where you will not be disturbed, and invite as many people as you possibly can from across the population affected by or interested in the subject.

OPENING	Introductions, Housekeeping, Expectations, Agenda, Ways of Working,
CLARITY	Context, definitions, clear contracting re outputs
IDEA GENERATION	Plenary, Groups, Maybe several linked exercises Use of co-facilitators
EXPLORATION & ANALYSIS	May use Neuland boards, flips, stickies etc / Facilitators questions, support, challenge and hold the boundaries
CONVERGENCE	Feedback, Presentations Tie back to theme Create Action Plans
CLOSURE	Next steps, farewells
FOCUS ON KEY OUTPUT	Poppyfish

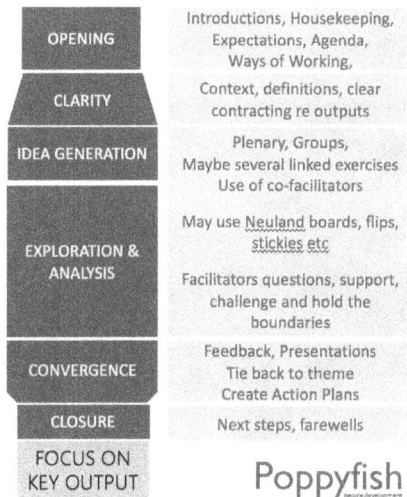

Facilitation Process – our lens

These sessions allow the people closest to a problem to work collaboratively to solve it. On the way they will share stories and experiences of their own that will enrich your own perspective, and which will create a body of evidence that you can act on, whether this is a deeper analysis of a problem, the scope for change, or a wild and wacky exploration of a new business idea. These sessions are super powerful. Use them in moderation, plan them well, and you will not regret the effort.

Diagonal Interviews

Alongside focus groups and workshops, diagonal interviews, that is, interviewing people from all parts of the business, give you a great indicator of how prevalent your issue is. Some projects that you work on will be very localized in nature. Others might be organization or even market wide. The key thing here is to speak to people from across the full scope of the issue, in terms of involvement, seniority, influence, and apparent interest. What you think is a local problem can be larger once you uncover all the evidence. Whenever we are engaged in any kind of change program we will always carry out diagonal interviews, normally on a one-to-one basis from across the business to get as broad a view as we can on the issue. And

Cosmetic

⬇

Conversational

⬇

Active

in those interviews, we ask a few questions but mainly we listen. And I mean we REALLY listen. What does that mean?

There are three levels of listening. Cosmetic listening, conversational listening, and active listening.

Cosmetic listening is the type of listening I engage in when I'm focused on something else. You might be chatting away but I'm still busy typing. I will nod and grunt at the right times but 10 minutes later I will have forgotten what you said. Conversational listening is what most of us engage in most of the time. We speak with people, exchanging words in a pattern to exchange information. We listen to the words but we don't always hear what's being said. How can we anyway, I mean we're probably in an open plan office, or on a bus, or in a car, or in a corridor, or in a street.

Active listening is a step up from conversational listening. When I am actively listening to you I am displaying all the skills of a great listener. We will be in a quiet and comfortable space with no distractions. I will be looking at you, I will be nodding my head to show I am listening, and I will be restating back to you what you just said so that you know that I understand it in the way that you meant it. And I'm doing more than that. I'm listening to the words you use and the language and metaphor that show me how you feel about something. I was conducting interviews with employees once who spoke of a change program as being an "asteroid" that was heading toward the business. That painted a pretty grim picture and one which we explored with some fascinating outcomes and insights that we later made use of in our change program communications. Generally, you are doing the talking, not me. After all, nobody ever learnt anything while they were talking, but I am prompting you with good open questions. Looking for evidence can depend on the type of questions that you ask. The best practice here is to ask great, open questions that remove much of your own agenda from the conversation.

If you want better answers, ask better questions. Questioning is one of the most important communication skills in all parts of life, and an essential skill for a good manager. Good communicators are able to ask questions that encourage others to feel comfortable in expressing themselves, without any feelings of judgment. By asking questions, you learn, you uncover problems and needs, and you demonstrate that the other person is important to you. This all contributes toward building a lasting relationship.

"Open" questions enable you to learn a lot about someone. You can grasp what the other person is thinking and feeling, explore what they value, and probe for more detail. They invite people to talk, to open up, to expand freely, and to stay engaged with you. Most importantly, open questions send the message that you are interested in more than a one-word reply. They are a plea for information and they seldom disappoint.

"Closed" questions, on the other hand, require only a limited response and can usually be answered with a simple "Yes" or "No." Closed questions can also lead the receiver toward a particular response, even unintentionally, so they can be leading questions.

If you are truly seeking evidence then you must choose your words very carefully, so as not to lead the other person into a particular answer. Humans are very good at asking people a question so that we receive the answer we want. For instance, when I say to my wife "Are you OK with staying in tonight?" what am I really saying? You could argue that I'm not really asking a question, but I am instead making a statement about what I would like.

As mentioned in the Opportunities chapter, asking a procession of open questions will allow you to delve deeply into a situation. Leadership expert Simon Sinek believes deeply in the power of why as a tool in leadership development. His TED talk on how leaders inspire action has almost 37 million views online, and if you haven't seen it I recommend it to you. But in evidence gathering we can look at one of the open questions that allows you to go swiftly to the heart of the matter.

Again we'd ask you to repeat the exercise from the opportunities section where we proposed using three open questions to get through the ice and into the real person at a networking event. In diagonal interviews we would say to repeat this practice, but with a target of five successive open questions. That is, ask one open question, and listen to a response, then, without judging and based on what you have heard, ask another open question in the area being discussed. Listen to the answer again and then ask another open question based on what you have heard, and listen again to the answer. Repeat this process, without any other form of intervention or question until you have asked five open questions. By now you will be really deep into the topic and your conversation will be more meaningful, more impactful, and more relevant as a consequence of this. It is not easy to do, because to do it well you have to actively listen to what the other person is saying and this is difficult. It's also difficult because often our brain yells at us "what question am I going to ask next," which actually stops us from hearing what is being said. But the more you do it, the better your outcomes will be, and you will have some fantastic conversations and be able to perform detailed inquiry and gain some insightful, applicable, and deeply personal evidence from people about how they see an issue.

Shadowing

Our third preferred way of gathering evidence is to see the situation for yourself. This can take many forms but shadowing an individual as they perform their role gives you a good insight into their daily struggle. If you are tasked with leading change then we highly recommend this practice to you. These work very well if accompanied with a diagonal interview, which is often best performed before the shadowing but can be equally effective afterward depending on what you are trying to gather evidence or learn about. Shadowing involves watching people at work and trying to be unobtrusive as you can. One thing you must be aware of, however, is the potential bias that can creep in through shadowing. There have been some very famous pieces of research looking at how people behave differently while they are being watched. But here's the clever thing. When you are shadowing one individual the rest of the office tends to relax and do its own thing. You can learn just as much, and sometimes more, by spending just as much time watching them out of the corner of your eye and absorbing the culture of that team, floor, or project. The learning can be just as applicable.

There's never enough time to gather enough evidence. The fact-finding phase of any project must be long enough to be meaningful but short enough to allow momentum to be maintained. And it's important to resource it. We were once asked to take over a change project that had been at the fact-finding stage for over 2 years. The reason for this was that it had been just part of somebody's job and they had other priorities. Within a week we had the project up on its feet again and completed the fact-finding stage over the next 6 weeks, not bad considering this was an international for a business.

Customer Feedback and NPS

For evidence about how your business is performing the best place to look is at your customers. On one level this is really easy, and it starts with what repeat business do you get? If people are coming back to you then that suggests that you are at least doing something right (celebrate the positives!) but there is more that can be done. Customer feedback matters, so, when you can, ask them that simplest of questions—how are we doing? How can we improve? It only takes a second to lose a customer but years to build loyalty so look after them. Customers can be keen to engage with suppliers if they feel that there is something they can get from the interaction. This can be anything from offering complementary events to focused customer workshops.

One way to measure your level of customer satisfaction is through NET PROMOTER SCORE or NPS: the feedback you get from your customers. NPS measures customer experience and predicts business growth. If the score ever goes below 7/10 then find out why, where, who can, and what to change it quickly.

Customer satisfaction surveys are normally standard templates and if you subscribe to an online survey company such as SurveyMonkey then you can access hundreds of good quality template surveys that can be used and edited to be specific and helpful to your business. But you can do it yourself simply by asking some simple and obvious questions. And also don't forget that although these days we would expect to do most of these activities online, there is still a place for telephone and even postal surveying (just bear in mind that the response rates for postal surveys can be less than 10 percent).

Here's a simple feedback form that you might use for an online retailer.

Customer Survey for ABC Online.

Please mark the following out of 10:

		Comments:
1. How happy are you with overall service you received from (name of your company)?	/10	
2. How would you rate the range of products available in our online catalog?	/10	
3. How happy were you with the quality of the item you received?	/10	
4. How would you rate aftercare/service you received after you had received your product?	/10	
6. How did you find our employees online/ face to face, etc.?	/10	
9. How likely are you to recommend our services to a friend?	/10	
Total scores	/100	Divide your total score by number of questions to give you your net promoter score

Please also read the comments and don't react straightaway but see if any patterns emerge and maybe don't ask every customer every time or it will annoy them. If we could give you one piece of evidence to help you increase your net promoter score it is to under promise and over deliver. If you surpass the expectations of others, then they will be more likely to rate you highly. But if you promise something and then fail to deliver against those promises, then you'll deserve a bad score, right? There is a furniture supplier in the UK whose NPS is high because they appear to be going the extra mile by surpassing your original expectations. When you order online or by telephone you get an immediate receipt by e-mail and a text saying your item will be delivered with 3 weeks. Then the next day customers often receive a message saying "we are delighted to say we can deliver sometime within 7 days." Then you choose a day and am or pm. Then they confirm it, text and e-mail you the day before confirming it again, give you the driver's name and mobile number, then the driver calls you at 9 am to give you a delivery time, and then he calls when he is 15 minutes away. They arrive, put it in a room of your choice in situ, remove packaging, take the unwanted packaging away, and make sure you are happy. And remember too the old saying that "customer service is not a department it is an attitude" and you can hear a smile down the phone line!

You can also look to your suppliers for their feedback, and this is especially true for the many companies that wish to be seen as treating their suppliers ethically and with reasonable payment terms and treatment. Going the extra mile for your supply chain is the mark of an ethically strong business, so pay them on time or early if you can, and remember without them you don't have a business.

Back to the Floor

Our last piece of evidence that great leaders can use to learn about their own business is back to the floor. You will hear us say many times in this book that your staff can tell you more about how to solve your problems than you already now—but only if you engage with them and ask them for help. If you can be a mystery shopper or ask a friend to do it for you, with specific questions in mind; or go back and work with the employees, do it. I have worked as a bin man, road sweeper, in a kitchen, manning the telephones in a call center, and any other roles for a day or two and learned more about the issues that the employees face than any board meeting and even better is at the breaks when you ask, what is it like to work here?

They WILL TELL YOU.

And there's one other thing you need to do with evidence, and that is present it back with conviction and with honesty. Do not make excuses or hide the feedback that you receive just because you are scared in case other people get upset or angry. The reason that you are uncovering the evidence is to take action so that improvements can be made, or new pathways identified. This book does not cover presentation skills, but if you can speak passionately, with purpose and with a good knowledge and understanding of the facts and reasoned implications of actions, then you are well on the way to delivering a potent and persuasive argument.

Remember these Golden Rules about Evidence

What we don't know we make up.

By asking better questions you can get better answers. Listening is a real skill, practice it.

Involving other people piques their interest and allows them to buy in to your cause.

Use focus groups, facilitated workshops, diagonal interviews, shadowing, customer feedback and NPS, and "back to the floor" to obtain evidence that will support your decision making and minimize the negative impact of your own biased view.

Time is important, don't allow yourselves to get bogged down in meaningless data collection. And don't be so arrogant as to think you know best! Other people know more than you.

CHAPTER 4

A Is for Actions

Can You Take Action When You Need To?

"Actions speak louder than words"

—proverb

"Your beliefs become your thoughts, your thoughts become your words, your words become your actions, your actions become your habits, your habits become your values, your values become your destiny."

—Mahatma Gandhi

So, you think you are ready to push the button on a new business or project? Before you do this, you're going to need to be sure that all the preparation is complete, and you have checked off all the Golden Rules from this book. And that includes making sure that you've got everything else you need in place to make your ideas work and stick.

The Best Way to Get a Job Done Is to Begin

There is a clever thinker active in the world of management science called Paul Kotter who wrote a seminal work on Leading Change in 1996. Kotter identified that there are eight things that you need to have in place before embarking on a change program (which we can also apply to launching a new venture). They are:

Create Urgency
Form a powerful coalition
Create a vision for change
Communicate the vision
Remove obstacles
Create Short-Term Wins
Build on the Change
Anchor the Changes in Corporate Culture

Create Urgency

This is normally by inducing a state of mild fear that the status quo is no longer supportable. Sometimes these urgencies are externally driven while at other times these can be created from within. The key skill here is influencing others and in persevering when you know you are right.

Form a Powerful Coalition

Who are the key stakeholders in this and who are the people who can influence and deliver this change? Making a stakeholder map is simple enough, just repeat the job map process from Chapter 4 but center the diagram around the project or idea rather than the job and you will create a map of people who have a vested interest in the outcome of your work. Keep your friends close and your enemies even closer—it is better to have them on the inside of your tent spitting out than to have them outside your tent spitting in!

Create a Vision for Change

Where are you going and why and what will the future be like? Check it with your disciples/coalition/friends and accept that there will be changes.

Communicate the Vision

Let others share your vision and they can help you achieve it. Physically do this; stand in front of your team and let them see the whites of your eyes. Tell a story of what the future will be like and outline the features' advantages and benefits. Be open about these and communicate them as early as you possibly can. Do not let your own fears for others prevent you from sharing whatever news you can. If you think there will be job losses, say so early. You cannot overcommunicate and whatever you do not tell people they will make up and these gaps are more likely to be painted in the negative ("why didn't he tell us? It must be bad news")

Remove Obstacles

We are going to focus a bit more closely on this one as there are some great tools that you can use to get to grips with this. Firstly, the identification of barriers is best done through consultation, not just through you making a guess. Ask all employees what is stopping us?

Forcefield is a useful tool to do this—it is a technique for identifying where you are today/now and where you want to be in any given time in the future, say 1 week, 1 month, or even at the end of this project and then analyzing the negative and positive factors in any given situation, known as driving and resisting forces which are either helping you or hindering your advancement in any given area. These are either the assets and strengths you have that can help you to achieve your aims or they are debits or blocks stopping you from moving forward. You then identify what actions could be taken and by whom and when (these are known as enablers) in order to build on the positives and thus make them even stronger or knock out the negatives.

Let's look at an example of how you might do this. Imagine you have been asked to lead the introduction of a new IT system for a business. The project has been proposed and the plan has been coming together really well. As part of your process you have brought the most critically affected people together to help make sure that you have buy in, support, and can hear their ideas on what needs to happen. As part of the day you have asked them to do a force field exercise to help them identify ways to overcome the perceived blocks to the project.

Firstly separate the pessimists from the optimists. People will often self-manage at this stage or you can fill a glass to the halfway point with water and ask if it is half full or half empty. Anyone who says half empty goes in the pessimist pile! It doesn't matter if the groups are slightly unequal, but you may have to ask a few people to swap if things look absurdly one-sided. Move the groups to separate sides of the room, or even into an anteroom, so they can speak without disturbing or influencing each other.

Then, go to the pessimist group and ask them to spend some time to agree to a list of the top six things that are blocking the project. You can do more but six works well and normally gives plenty of material to work with. It's up to you really how many you choose to look at. These are the barriers to the project goals being secured. They may be of any type: physical, mental, real, or perceived. Ask them to write each one on a separate sheet of paper, card, or large sticky note so that, when their thinking time is up, they can be displayed to the entire group to create a brick pattern like the one below. The positions of each brick in the wall don't matter.

What you should end up with is a wall, facilitation board, or flip chart that looks a bit like this (obviously the individual blockers on your project will be different):

As soon as you have briefed the pessimistic team as to their task, give the optimists their brief (so that the teams work at the same time). Again, make sure they are not too close to the pessimists so that the groups interfere or disturb each other's thinking. Ask this group to come up with a list of strengths or drivers that are supporting you or will help you to achieve your project outcomes. Again, ask them to agree to these top six strengths and write each one on a paper or card in the same style as the pessimists. Once done, this can also be displayed on the same wall, but positioned in a way that is below the blockers and pointing toward it.

What you should now have is a group back in plenary and looking at a wall that looks a bit like this:

Now comes the fun part. Divide the group into six, assigning one of the blockers to each group. Ask them to agree to some actions that can be taken to overcome that block using the strengths identified. There could

Fear of change	Too much other work	High staff turnover
Tiny budget	Poor IT skills	Outdated Processes

Blockers that stand between us and our goal

Strong technical skills

Supportive clients

New people have energy!

Great comms team

Good leadership

Top team want change

Things that will help us succeed in our goal (our strengths and drivers)

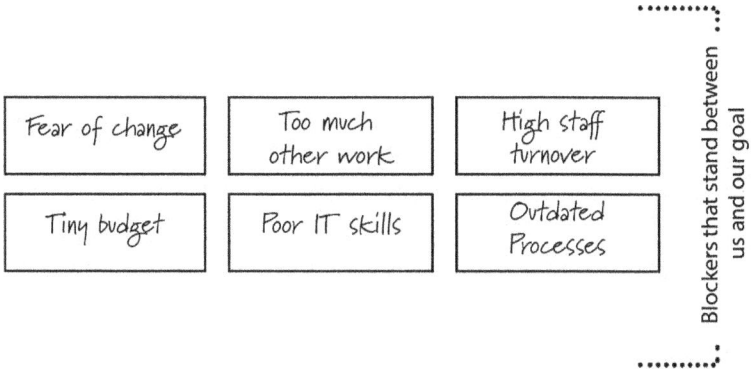

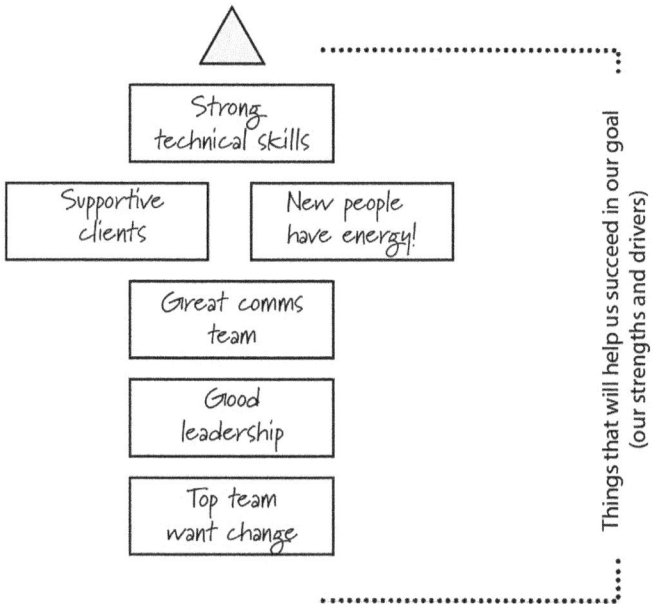

be just one action per block, or there could be more than one. Once more, capture these actions (in pure Forcefield these are called enablers), maybe using a different colored card or paper. At the end of this exercise your wall should look something like this:

Fear of change
Allow hands on sessions
Demonstrate benefits early
Reassure people that job is safe

Too much other work
Outsource KKTV project

High staff turnover
Provide training & support
Communicate new structure
Show a clear career path

Poor IT skills
Comms team to make training videos
Recruit IT trainer for 6 mths

Tiny budget
Lobby leadership for extra £100K

Outdated Processes
Listen to new people

Strong technical skills

Supportive clients

New people have energy!

Great comms team

Good leadership

Top team want change

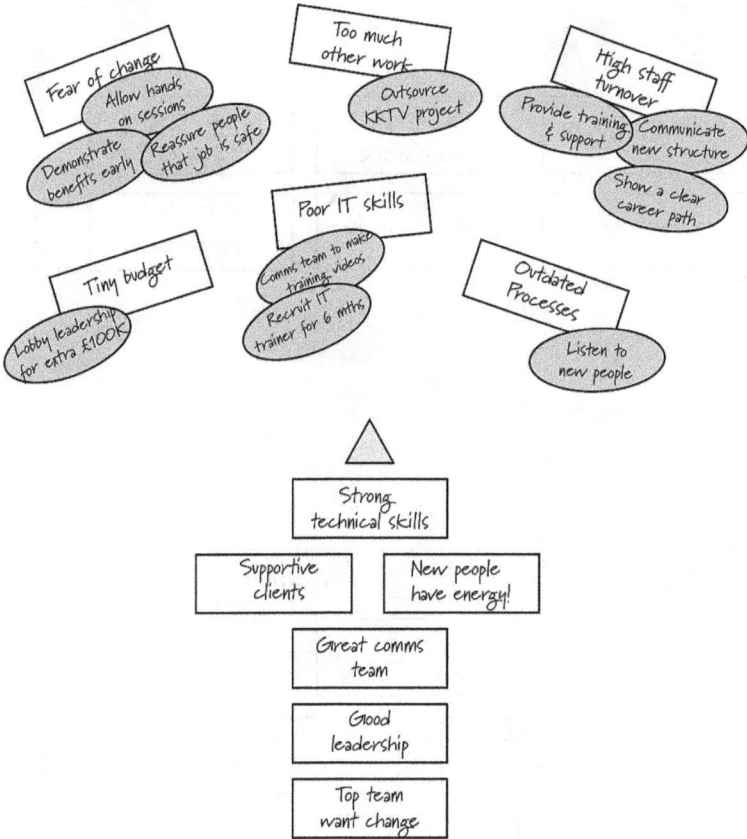

By doing this not only have you identified the barriers but you have also, within the space of the same group session, targeted them and agreed the manner in which they can be overcome. What you have created here is a list of actions, created by consensus, that will help your project move forward. You can keep this exercise simple, or you can make it a longer and deeper dive in which you can explore all of the issues raised. And you can do it in one session with one group or repeat it over a number of sessions with a number of groups. The more groups you can do this with the more confident you can be of the outputs. Of course, by doing this you are also shining a little light into culture as you are getting an insight of what it is really like to work in your business or team. Share the outputs of this session and invite others to comment. Feed them back up the hierarchy and let other see how effective this tool is.

As the leader of the process the next stage is really important, and it is that you must take action on the ideas raised and show progress. Only a fool would go through this process and then not act on the issues raised; however, there may be some that have to be turned down. If so you must make sure that you have a really good reason for this and you must communicate those reasons to the team.

Another technique for removing obstacle is to use a metaphor of the old left versus right brain theory first published by the *New York Times* in 1973—although much of this was argued against and has been disproved in terms of the neuroscience in the physical sense, this approach still stands as a metaphor for understanding behavior and with unblocking blocks.

Imagine all your thinking patterns happen like this, with one side of your mind being decisive, logical, good with numbers, good with words, scientific, controlling, needing proof and reason, realism, and order and timings, while the other side of your mind is intuitive, emotional, dreamy, artistic, random, happy to go with the flow, imaginative, creative, and musical. The left side deals with facts and numbers and evidence, while the right side talks about "always" and "never."

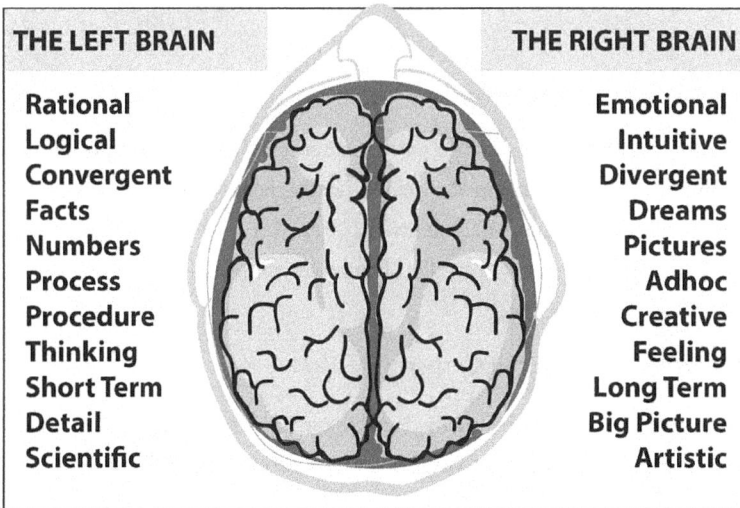

THE LEFT BRAIN		THE RIGHT BRAIN
Rational		Emotional
Logical		Intuitive
Convergent		Divergent
Facts		Dreams
Numbers		Pictures
Process		Adhoc
Procedure		Creative
Thinking		Feeling
Short Term		Long Term
Detail		Big Picture
Scientific		Artistic

Left and Right Brain Metaphor

Now imagine a block—and decide where the block comes from—which side is it more closely related to? Then look on the other side for a solution—here are a few to get you started.

Left Brain Block	Right Brain Solution
"We can't go on holiday. We can't afford it, there's nobody to look after the dog, it's too far to the airport, I get airsick and we've got no suitcases."	"just *imagine* what it will feel like to be on that beach."

Right Brain Block	Left Brain Solution
"We can't win with this. The marketing department *always* let us down and *never* give us anything on time."	"In two years of dealing with them we have received 16 pieces of work from them of which 2 have been late. Is it really an issue?"

Use this tips and you will find the action can win over the blocks.

Create Short-Term Wins

Write easy SMART goals for week one and have a reward ready—a beer after work, a meal, pay for lunch to be brought in—a small simple way to celebrate the first successes. This is a really good method of overcoming procrastination, that most feared enemy of action and about which we will talk in a minute.

Build on the Change

When a small piece of change has been achieved ask the person who did it—what are you going to do next? Get them to write their own smart goals and present them to you so that you don't have to keep thinking about the next goals for everyone. Empower them.

Anchor the Changes in Corporate Culture

Keep your business plan up-to-date by writing the changes in it weekly or monthly so it evolves as you do. Let it become a live diary so you can look back and look forward.

Our experience tells us that Kotter's thinking is well founded and makes a lot of sense. These actions make positive outcomes more likely and are overlooked at your peril. The unstated but rather obvious emphasis on all of these is actually DOING it and to keep DOING it. We find in organizational change programs that people view Kotter as a tick list. Have I created urgency? Check. Have I formed a powerful coalition? Check. People work through these in succession and when they move on to the next one they forget the previous one. It doesn't work like that. You don't target these areas one at a time, you target many of them at once and some of them are always live. In our practical experience realizing this is key. It's not just about one action, it's about all actions. For instance, when it comes to big whole organization change programs there is usually a lengthy timeline. Outlining and communicating the vision is not just something you do at the start, it needs to be in people's eye line all the time and updated and refreshed. The barriers to change will rise and fall in different areas at different times. The guiding coalition will change as the project goes through different phases, and the list of short-term wins can be the only thing that signals progress. Active management is required.

So, while planning ahead is crucially important, you cannot allow that planning to freeze action. You must get started.

With any project or plan you're going to need a timeline. This can be anything from a collection of post-it notes stuck on a wall to a fancy Gantt chart with responsibilities and dependencies using some fancy project management software.[1]

The timeline or project plan can be developed to whatever depth you need to work in the organization that you are in and with the people you have got. That may sound like a cop out, but this is not a one-size-fits-all solution. Under some methodologies you will be required to have precise work breakdown structures, Gantt charts, and critical path analysis, the gory details of which we do not have the space to go into here.

---

[1]Over the years by far the most useful and helpful project management software we have used is Microsoft Project. It is well worth getting a copy if you are stepping into any project management or planning role.

These tools serve three key aims:

1. They help you to plan what you are going to do and when
2. They help you to know what resources you will need and when
3. They help you to demonstrate what you have completed and how far you still have to go.

So, whether you are building a house, or embarking on a software project, or even just redesigning and rebuilding your kitchen you'll need some kind of plan. And more importantly you'll need someone who is action orientated to lead it (and if you are reading this book that's probably you by the way). Because while the plan is crucial the good project manager or leader doesn't spend all day at his screen working on updating schedules and creating reports. The bad news is that s/he will have to do that but it's not his or her ability at doing that which will win the day. What will win the day is in their ability to manage Kotter's eight principles and make stuff happen.

Fighting Off the Procrastination Bug

Let's be honest, scheduling actions is easy. Or at least it is if you're the type who's organized, self-disciplined, and already have a great record of getting things done, but for the rest of us sometimes it's hard to get started. Even though we know we should. What's needed is self-discipline and a little bit of stress. Time management (which we will look at in the next chapter to some degree) and persistence are two types of fuel for cultivating self-discipline, and a little bit of stress keeps you sharp. I don't mean negative stress, but an application of positive stress, that moment when you step into gear and have that extra glint in your eye.

Stress can be a positive driver for change, it's only when you tip over into distress that the problems start to come. Some positive stress, applied when needed, is enough to get that project over the line. "I love the smell of deadlines in the morning," as one of my mentors once said. That little bit of positive stress can give you energy and drive and help you make effective use of your time and avoid distractions. If you waste time and allow yourself to get distracted in progressing toward your desired goal, you welcome unsuccessful habits instead of successful ones.

Tackling Procrastination

Nothing drives action like an approaching deadline, and for some of us the rapid approach of the crisis moment is just about the only thing that can spur action. One of the biggest issues with procrastination is not the task itself but the issue of negativity that goes with it. So for instance when I get a toothache and know that I should go to the dentist I get into a spiral of negative thinking that goes a bit like this:

> Procrastinating me: "Ow! My tooth is hurting, that's going to cost me a fortune and I'll probably need a filling and then they'll take it out and my face will hurt and I'll dribble all afternoon, and I'll probably have to take time off work to go, and you can never park at that surgery."

In just a second or two I have racked up enough negativity about going to the dentist to make sure that I don't revisit that thought for a while, there's just too much there to cope with. So what can I do to help me take the action I should take in the first place and phone the dentist? How about this? What I can do is, instead of focusing on the negative and depressing aspects of the problem, I play my action-oriented thinker card and say: what's the outcome I need to resolve this? I need to get my tooth fixed. With this worked out I can then instigate the first step of an action that will get me to that outcome—book a slot with the dentist. Once that step is made I have done the hard part, and I'm on the way to getting my tooth fixed because once the action is committed then I'm happy I can just hold to schedule. So, if I re-run the dialogue inside my head it might go something like this:

> "Ow, my tooth hurts. I need to get that fixed. I'll phone now and get an appointment."

Taking this approach requires rewiring your brain, but like any behavioral change once you are aware of it you will find yourself recrafting conversations in your head to make the change happen. At first this will feel really odd and uncomfortable, but over time that discomfort will settle, and if you can make a habit of the new way of thinking then you can make real inroads to making a change for the better.

If you feel that procrastination is an issue for you then there are some good approaches, like the one above, that can help you. Here's another very simple one to get you started on a piece of work that you have been putting off.

1. Schedule 1 hour in your diary.
2. Get a timer, and at the start of the hour set the timer for 30 minutes.
3. Work on the task for 30 minutes with NO DISTRACTIONS.
4. After 30 minutes the timer will go off and you have an option. You can either (a) reward yourself with 30 minutes of free time or (b) work on the task for another 30 minutes.
5. At the end of that hour, schedule another hour later the next day and repeat the sequence.

Remember These Golden Rules about Action

Doing something is always preferable to doing nothing.
Kotter's eight principles work. Use them.
You don't have to do it all yourself, involve others as soon as possible.
An action that gets scheduled gets done.

CHAPTER 5

T Is for Timings

Can You Get Your Timings Right and Do Things before It's Too Late?

"Patience is power. Patience is not an absence of action; rather it is 'timing' it waits on the right time to act, for the right principles and in the right way."

—Fulton J Sheen

Timing is all about the choice, the judgment, or control of when something should be done. It's also about where you are and when and the things that you should do regularly. This chapter looks at timeliness, time management matrixes, to do lists, and mindfulness. The value of content here, we hope, is in the combination of possible tools and techniques to help you feel more in control of events, instead of feeling at their mercy. Here's a few home truths about time management and getting things done:

Things always take longer than you expect.

You can be in the right place at the right time.

Sheer laziness is the top contributor to lost productivity.

Meetings are just an excuse not to work.

Activity is not the same as achievement.

Once you can face and accept these truths you are already on the way to improving your effectiveness and your timings.

If the 80/20 rule is right, then 20 percent of your time at work produces 80 percent of your output. That means that you might only get

96 minutes of productive time in an 8-hour working day. When you look at it like that it's amazing that anybody ever gets anything done. It's no surprise then that we are obsessed with getting more and more productive. The good news though is that on the same basis, 20 percent of our interventions will solve 80 percent of our worries—we just have to pick the right intervention!

The Planning Fallacy

Human beings are incredibly bad at calculating how long it takes to do things. We all know this, and yet somehow we create difficulties for ourselves by always underestimating what needs to be done, be that a project goal or a physical destination. I know I can run 100 meters in 12 seconds, so running 400 meters takes 48 seconds. No, it doesn't. Scaling up multiple instances of interrelated activities is not linear. Just because I can eat one chocolate bar in 10 seconds and one marshmallow in 5 doesn't mean that you can, and it certainly doesn't mean that I can eat four chocolate bars and four marshmallows in 1 minute. The handover element of interrelated tasks is one of the prime reasons that 90 percent of railroad construction projects overrun. Our experience in software development and construction in the UK suggests that software product development typically lags behind plan by anything up to 30 percent and construction projects slip by at least 1 to 2 days a week. Often in these instances, in construction in particular, it's not the individual tasks that are the challenge but the gaps in-between. I know that the tiler will take 3 days, and the decorating 2 days, but a 5-day completion for the job requires an instant handover between the two. Seldom does it work like that. What happens is the tiler finishes at midday on Tuesday and the decorator, who wants to ensure the tiles are set before he starts his work, gets underway on Thursday morning (and besides, he can't get there sooner as he's still finishing a job on the far side of town). We all know about these delays in baton handovers, yet despite us all knowing this to be true we still subconsciously overlook this and commit ourselves to deadlines that will never be hit on time. It took the 1979 work of Daniel Kahneman and Amos Tversky to put some psychological reasoning behind this phenomenon.

One way to combat the planning fallacy (because you will never totally avoid it) is to use data from comparable efforts. Past performance is a great indicator of future performance, just ask anyone who studies "the form" in horse racing. Looking at how a horse ran on its last three races in similar conditions might give you an idea of how it will run in the next race.

There's lots of uncertainty around this, but most people can tell the likely winners from the donkeys. This carries across into business, where simple starting point can be historical projects. How did it go last time you did this? Few companies look back to see how well past forecasts panned out, let alone seek to understand the markers that identify successful projects. It's why reviews, which we look at in their own right in the third volume of our Blood, Sweat and Tears trilogy are so vital.

Incidentally, it's tempting to think that I can get you to work faster if I give you a performance bonus based on your ability to deliver on time. Research however suggests that if this task requires any cognitive effort what-soever (i.e., it involves problem solving or creative thinking or collaborative effort or innovation or change), that this bonus will not improve output in any way, and might actually make the output slower or worse, and maybe both.

Running Premortems and the 3-Obstacles Test

A postmortem is an investigation that is carried out after death, to explain the reasons behind the demise. In our line of work we call these "post-project reviews." We don't do enough of them, but when we do we can learn a lot about what went wrong on a project, and apply that on the next project. It's helpful for the next project but it doesn't help the one that's just started. We work with clients on premortems, that is, looking ahead at what will kill the project before it starts, rather than after it has ended. The reasons for this are surprisingly obvious. Most of us who have been around the block a few times have an idea of the likely blockers to a successful outcome. We know in advance that we will have recruitment delays, supply problems, poor weather, illness, etc., etc., and that these will all serve to delay the pace of work and threaten (by which I really mean "miss") deadlines. Premortems bring the various stakeholders together to share the reasons why the project WILL go wrong. It may sound pessimistic but all we are doing here is acknowledging the existence of the planning fallacy and trying to negate the impact of it on your project or strategic plan. We tend to work these as facilitated group sessions where concerns and worries get aired. The reason they work so well is that they allow you to recognize a few crucial things:

A) Some obvious problems can be easily side-stepped with planning
B) That expectations exchanges between parties help people to work together more effectively as they already have a shared understanding that makes future communication easier and gets the project off to a good start
C) You can spot early warning signs of failure and have a preagreed plan of how to act
D) That bringing stakeholders together really works
E) They build engagement, accountability, and trust

When running premortems, or with any review of timings, there is always the tendency to discount previous experience because that was a "special set of circumstances." Kahneman and Tversky also highlighted this as just one reason why we repeatedly fall foul of the fallacy. We reflect on what happened and say that it was a special or unpredictable event, which of course it almost definitely wasn't. And there is a pattern in this which is also about protecting ourselves from criticism. As humans we have a tendency to believe that when things go wrong it is because of something that someone else did to us or that which was outside our control. Similarly we often state that when something went right, it was because of something we did. We like to use the exercise below to ask people to think differently about this:

Are we really the ones that deserve the credit?

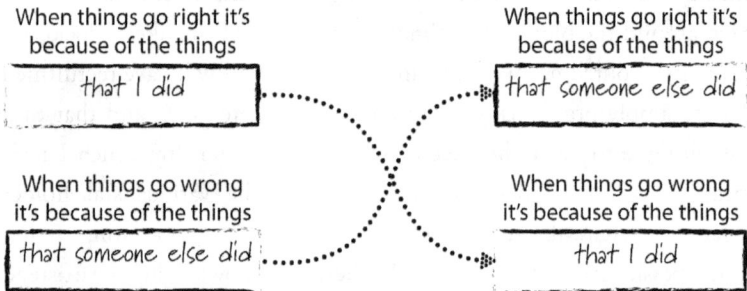

When things go right it's because of the things	When things go right it's because of the things
that I did	that someone else did

When things go wrong it's because of the things	When things go wrong it's because of the things
that someone else did	that I did

If you think honestly for a few moments how many of us can't say that we prefer to see things as they appear on the left? If you want to see examples of this just watch some postmatch interviews with sports managers and coaches—especially UK Premier League teams. They say things like "I played Jessie down the left wing because I knew his speed would be too much for the defenders to match" followed almost immediately by "And the referee made a bad decision which cost us the game." This is a defense mechanism for feeling bad. What might be more honest would be "Their goal came when they exploited the gap that Jessie left on the left wing, I should have reshuffled the defence to allow for that" The latter sounds more mature, but the first sounds more recognizable.

We are not advocating turning things around like this at all times, but be aware of the propensity that we all have to project information in this way. Swapping the phrases around and looking at the story from the other side can give you a refreshingly novel view and can allow people to have a more honest discussion about what needs to be different or better. And when you hear project managers telling you about all the things that they did that created a great outcome, despite all the things that went wrong that they could not foresee or control, just try turning the phrase around.

The 3-obstacles test is another simple exercise that can be included in a premortem or is equally credible as a stand-alone exercise to combat the planning fallacy. When calculating the duration of any task, scientists have shown[1] that you can engage more conscious thinking and get more accurate assessments of times and outputs simply by asking what three obstacles stand in my way of achieving this goal? This then enables you to plan how they may be overcome and what resources you will need, and gives you a more reasonable view of the likely time and cost required for solution. Many project planners will tell you they always circumvent these problems. The truth is they don't. "Friction" is always out there. This period of reflectiveness and critical thinking is enough to improve your time estimates.

Timings: Time Management

Time is precious. We all know that and yet many of us manage to find a way to waste it. We manage to find things to do that cost us time but give little

---

[1]Sanna and Schwarz, 2004.

gain. And we don't have to travel far from home to find those time-wasting opportunities. Indeed, many of them are in our own homes: the TV, the Xbox, the Internet. You see, the attractions of modern life make it so easy for us to waste our time, to fill large chunks of our leisure time with nothing in particular but in a way that makes it seem like we're having fun.

Now, I'm no time management angel. I have all the same time management issues as the next man, but the fact is that I know that how I spend my time is a choice. I can choose to relax and spend my time scratching my backside while watching old John Wayne films, or I can choose to do something that might be more likely to improve my life, or to improve the lives of others.

Maybe that would include spending time on self-development or learning a new skill. When I propose to people who attend our workshops that this choice exists, many look blank. Often, they argue that choice or not, they do not have enough free time in the week to put into doing something different. These excuses deny us the opportunity to learn something new for ourselves.

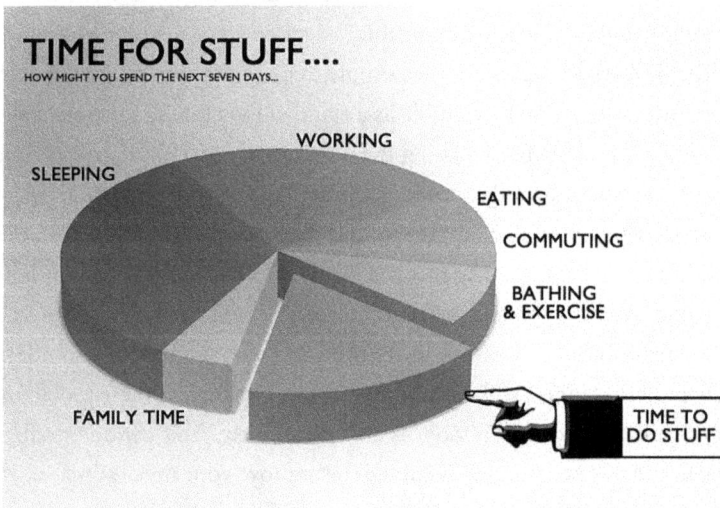

TIME FOR STUFF....
HOW MIGHT YOU SPEND THE NEXT SEVEN DAYS...

WORKING

SLEEPING

EATING

COMMUTING

BATHING & EXERCISE

FAMILY TIME

TIME TO DO STUFF

Because I would argue that there is time, if you make it. Look at the graph. Even if I am working a 40-hour week and have family ties there is still time in the week to make a difference—maybe as much as 30 hours even with all the other stuff that has to be done. And that's a good chunk of serious minutes. It might not be as much as you would like, but it's up to you what you make of it. We make time for the things and the people that we enjoy.

We're back to the 80/20 rule. You spend 20 percent of your day producing 80 percent of your outcomes. We'd like you to feel more productive and generate more time for stuff so here are a few tips to improve your time management, starting with something we call the Time Management check in process.

Time Management Check In

This does exactly what it says on the tin. You basically plan and review in tiny steps as you go through the day. Lots of us do this already on a mental level but the idea here is that you do it on a physical level, focusing directly on each phase as you do it. The principle is based around little and often. It's easy and forms good habits. The idea is that you manage each day as though it were its own project using a process that look like this:

Step One (5 minutes): Set your plan for the day. What are your top tasks that must be completed? What did you learn from yesterday? You can use one of the techniques later in this chapter to help you manage this part of the process.

Step Two (1 minute every hour): Refocus your plan. Keep on track.

Step Three (5 minutes): Review your day. Learn from what happened. Think about tomorrow.

Magic Hour

Magic Hour is a time management tool designed to ensure that you always give yourself time for the important stuff. Following on from the previous chapter this may be when you want to reflect on some of those actions that remain outstanding. The principle is an hour every day to sit back and reflect on where are we, how far have we come since yesterday, and prioritize your actions. To do this mark out 8 am to 9 am every day to hang the "do not disturb" sign on your locked door, sit with a coffee and check that everything others said they would do they have and what you said you would do you have. You can check all e-mails, read the post, make phone calls, and look at your priorities list.

I have a page in my diary something like this:

Item no.	Issue, Goal, Objective, Target, To Do, etc.	Next action or closed
1	Talk to Bill about new printer and training to use the scanner	Done
2	Invite suppliers to talk about lowering their costs if we order more less frequently saving on transport?	Ask Lynne to organize for tomorrow
3	Pay all invoices tomorrow	Carry forward to Friday 2 pm

Then, as part of magic hour you can schedule these to be completed. What gets scheduled gets done.

To prioritize simply look at these 4 boxes and decide.

I M P O R T A N C E	High importance/Low Urgency Do it later on today	High Urgency and High Importance Do it today! Do it now! Do not delay!
	Medium Importance/Low Urgency Do it in a few days	Medium Importance/High Urgency Do it later on today
	Low Importance/Low Urgency Delegate or forget	High Urgency/Low Importance Delegate it
Low	Medium	High
URGENCY		

When working with To Do lists it is good to remember to only schedule part of your day (because you will get interruptions and people always fall victim to the planning fallacy). Remember also to use blocks of time and kill first things first and in small batches (as for curbing procrastination).

The ABCD Method

Perfect for managers with lots of red in their profile. Most of our time we are busy busy busy, but the outputs are not great. Sometimes less is more. You can take a very direct "less is more" approach to your to do list by only focusing on accomplishing the things that matter with the ABCD method. Firstly write out your to do list, then go down the list marking items with A, B, C, or D as follows:

A—things that must be done today

B—things that must be done in the next 2 to 3 days

C—things that you need to do but which are not urgent

D—things you'd like to do

The next stage is simple: Do the A's, schedule the B's, and forget the rest!

Where You Are and When: Mindfulness for Managers

Timings is also about where you are and when. And what we mean by that is, you cannot be in two places at once, and you cannot multitask. When you are in a senior and/or pressured position you will often feel, no matter where you actually are, that you should be somewhere else. This can happen at different levels. You can be in one meeting and feel that you should be with another. You can be with your accountant and feel that you should be with a client. You can be with a client and feel that you should be working on that presentation that you've got to give tomorrow, you can be with you work colleagues and feel that you should be with your family, and you can be with your family and feel you should be at work. These are common conditions and are feelings that we've probably all experienced from time to time.

There's another fact that goes alongside this. For as well as only being able to be in any one place at any one time, it's also impossible to do more than one thing at a time. Forget all the multitasking mumbo-jumbo, it's just not possible to multitask. You can do things rapidly one after the other, and flit from task A to task B but you cannot actually multitask. When you sleep, you're asleep. When you drink water you drink. You can't sleep and drink a glass of water at the same time. If you tried it you'd look foolish, make a mess, and probably injure yourself. It's no different in business.

The modern manager faces so many distractions that it is hard to be focused in the here and now, to be "mindful" and "present." Our phones are always on, receiving calls, SMS texts, facetime calls, WhatsApp messages, social media updates, e-mails, delivery notifications, newsflashes, weather updates, the list is almost endless. And with technology going the way it is then there will soon be nowhere to hide. Only there is always somewhere to hide, you just have to find it. But this increasingly invasive world in which we live can dictate the pace with which you live your life. If you are to succeed in this role without becoming absurdly stretched and stressed then you will need to develop some way of focusing, and closing that world out now and then. This could be through time management techniques that allow you to organize your time in the most precise way, it could be by using a "magic hour" to reflect, prioritizes, and focus on key issues and problems, it could be by employing a superb personal assistant to do these things for you, or it could be a more spiritual focus that you adopt through meditation or yoga. You might not do all of them, and some will sound more attractive than others, but the truth is that if you currently don't do ANY of them, then you're going to struggle. We'd advise trialing them all and then finding a mix that works for you.

Getting Started with Being Present

Draw a deep breath in through your mouth. Hold it a moment, then let it out through your nose. The mouth and the nose are "wired" slightly differently. When you breathe out through your nose you stimulate a relaxation response from your body. As the breath goes out you feel the air dropping away, and will feel a settling sensation, a little like you are easing into a chair (that's because you always breathe out when you sit down). Feel that breath. And then do it again. What does it feel like? Well, it feels like being present, because in those few moments your focus was on nothing else. No distractions, no work stresses, no futile attempts at multitasking, and no dashing to collect the kids. Just breathing. And your heart rate dropped slightly. Congratulations, you just meditated.

Mindfulness is the mental state of being engaged in the now without emotionally reacting to our thoughts. Supporters of mindfulness claim it improves social relationships, communication, and empathic concern toward others. It's a clear presence of mind that helps you focus more effectively on what matters most. It helps to get more done, more easily, more effectively, and more enjoyably. And it's good for self-control. It's a process in which you can be in the present 100 percent, with no drawings to the past or the future. You are simply right here, right now. And focused.

We've seen rising interest in businesses wishing to cultivate moment-to-moment awareness and mindfulness in the workplace and such initiative can sit at the center of well-being campaigns aimed at reducing stress at work. But does it work?

Berkeley University conducted a study that looked at 96 supervisors and their subordinates from a variety of industries. The study looked at measuring the level of mindfulness in the supervisor as well as examining their employees' emotional exhaustion, work–life balance, and overall job performance. The research found that the more mindful the leader, the lower the employee's emotional exhaustion. Leader mindfulness was also associated with better work–life balance for the employee and better overall job performance ratings of the employee. A later study also found that the more mindful the manager, the more likely the employee was to engage in good citizenship, such as showing concern toward coworkers and expressing opinions honestly. Interestingly this research also suggested this only happened once basic needs (Maslow again) had been met.

Here are a few simple techniques that create mindfulness that you can incorporate at work:

Spend at least 5 minutes each day doing nothing (absolutely nothing). Just focus on your breathing. If you find it too stressful to be separated from your phone for that long you'll be pleased to know that there are some apps that you can download to help with this. Try some. Or try paying attention to your walking by slowing your pace and feeling the ground against your feet. Try walking with your eyes closed—you will be forced to use all your senses to stay safe (make sure you choose a safe location to do this with no dangerous hazards or risks). Or take time out through the day to get in touch with your senses by noticing the temperature of your skin and background sounds around you. Another idea is to eat a cookie, slowly over 5 minutes, feeling the biscuit, and tasting it slowly. If this sounds nuts just try it. These techniques allow your mind to focus on the here and now, and this can help you retain focus and mental discipline at work that will improve your effectiveness. By practicing these things you can create mindfulness triggers. Pick some everyday things that you do routinely. Decide that whenever you do them you will be mindful and will be aware that you are doing them. These might be climbing the stairs, eating a cookie, taking a shower. Then maybe try it when you're in a meeting, totally focused, totally present, and 100 percent in the here and now.

Remember These Golden Rules about Timings and Time Management

Remember the planning fallacy. You can't eat six chocolate bars in a minute.

You can't do everything! Use the Urgent/Important Matrix to help you determine what needs to be done.

Be flexible. Allow for contingency time. You'll be glad you did. It's not what you DO—It's what you DON'T do

Know your distractions and reward yourself for not being tempted by them.

Ask yourself: How is this moving me toward my goal?

Break goals down into smaller tasks and move forward bit by bit. Keep your eye on where you are headed. Replan when necessary.

Don't waste time on jobs no one expects you to do. Keep in the common ground. It's your responsibility. No one else really cares what you do. They are all fighting their own battles.

And remember,

ONLY A FOOL BREAKS THE TWO-MINUTE RULE!

Sometimes you just have to get on and do it. If you can do it in 2 minutes then it might just be best to get it done . . . with caution!

CHAPTER 6

And Is for

"And Don't Forget Your Family and Friends!"

"No one wants their grave stone to read—'I wish I'd spent longer at work!'"

—Anonymous

You have a tough life. You work hard. You focus on brand, you lead your team in accordance to their needs and set a great personal example, you set goals for your business and your teams and you measure outcomes. You assess and juggle with opportunities, you make tough decisions, you think about and communicate strategic direction. You think about "What if . . ." and look for evidence before taking action. You work hard on timings and being present. You spend time in training sessions and planning self-development, you encourage those around you to excel, your communicate announcements clearly and in the right spirit, you review everything you do to ensure that you are always delivering against your goals. You do all this and you are known for your success.

You must be exhausted.

The most important resources in your business are the people who work in it. The single most important business resource in your own business life is you. And you are no good to anybody if you are suffering negative stress and burnout. Working without a break is bad for your business, bad for your relationships, and bad for your health. While positive stress can be good for you, enabling you to step up and play at your best, negative stress or distress is debilitating and unhealthy. Stress is usually used to describe the feelings that people experience when the demands made on them are greater than their ability to cope. At such times people can often feel overloaded, under tremendous pressure, and very tense or emotional. It's not a good place to be. There are many warning signs of stress. Most importantly, do not ignore the early warning signs of stress; excessive irritability, prolonged bouts of anger and negativity, decreased sex drive, excessive emotions, lack of focus, overeating (also undereating), disturbed sleep, increased use of alcohol and tobacco product, a feeling of just being swamped are all signs. If you recognize any of those conditions then our advice is to speak to colleagues, friends, and family and be open and honest in those conversations. Analyze the cause of the stress and always seek appropriate medical help when needed.

At the end of the day what you do with your body is your business. You are an adult and you know the benefits of healthy eating, exercise, and the devils of drink—both excessive alcohol and caffeine can cause problems. But among all your work challenges be sure to work some "me" time into your schedule. All work and no play makes for a dull life. Make this me time habitual to maximize your chances of keeping to it. Have a hobby, play sports, listen to music, read classic literature and fiction, write poetry, walk the dog, take a city break, do voluntary community work, whatever takes your fancy. It diverts the mind and stimulates creativity and if it involves physical movement then that's even better. A great way to keep the mind stimulated and yet relaxing at the same time is to learn a new skill like ballroom dancing or how to fly. These are great escapes and will allow you to come back into work feeling refreshed.

Family time can keep you sane and is good for you. If you have a family then you must take quality time which you can spend alone, or with a loved one, or with friends and receive undivided attention, in such a way as to strengthen the relationship. Even if you feel you don't need this, they do! To enjoy the time when you are not working doing something you love to do.

Sleep keeps you healthy and your brain fresh. Monitor your sleeping pattern (many fitness trackers allow you to do this and they are getting more accurate) and ensure you get 8 hours of sleep. Most of the people who claim that they can get by on 4 hours sleep are probably lying or already dead.

Be altruistic and give something back to society. Individuals who report a greater interest in helping others are more likely to rate themselves as happy. Allow yourself time to recognize how your role gives something back to your community, and enjoy that involvement.

Remember too that nobody ever truly achieved anything on their own. To succeed in your dreams you will need the support of others who will influence your life and how you lead it. Those people matter. Some will be family, some will be friends, some will be friends who feel like family. Choose those people who make you feel that way you want to feel.

Remember the saying "If you want to fly with the eagles, don't hang around with turkeys." Nurture the relationships that matter, and do not encourage negative people into your life. Nobody likes a "mood hoover" or a "psychic vampire"—people who suck the life out of a room or conversation the moment they enter it. Keep away from these people.

Steve Head is a specialist High Performance Coach in the UK. His book, "How to avoid a near life experience" is short, simple, honest, and simply excellent for anyone who wants to follow their dreams. Head is a major advocate of the importance of your support network (or Dream Team) as he calls it. He states that building your own network requires TIME. The T stands for Trust, the core ingredient in any relationship. The I is for Integrity, someone who lives by strong values. The M is for Mutual benefit, a belief in the win–win aspect of the relationship. E is for Empathy, for they must be in touch with their emotions and be able to see the world through the eyes of others.

It's a good model, and one we'd encourage you to think about.

CHAPTER 7

Conclusions on SWEAT

"I am slowly coming to the conclusion that it's more important to learn to work with what you've got, under the circumstances you've been given, than wishing for different ones."

—Charlotte Eriksson

This book, the second volume in our trilogy, has asked you to consider some fundamental issues. We started with a major concept: STRATEGY. Having a business strategy defines the path of your business. Having a personal strategy defines your journey as a human. We saw that strategy links strongly to brand, leadership, and many of the other concepts that we saw in the first volume of this book, BLOOD. These linkages reinforce the lived reality that none of the concepts and situations that we discuss in this book exist in isolation. In truth these concepts exist as a delicate web of linked situations and approaches. As a manager or leader, the actions that you take in one area will create intended and unintended consequences in other linked areas. Exactly what outcomes they may be can be hard, even impossible to predict. But take action you must, for the alternative to action is inaction, which is the first step on the road to failure.

At the close of this second volume, it's important that we restate some of the core principles that we believe will help you make the most of our offering.

Firstly, **accept yourself as data**. Your experiences are valid. The thoughts, feelings, and experiences that you have are yours and are real. Don't be dictated by others (and yes, there is a certain irony in even writing that in a list of tips!). Take as much information as you can from situations. Reflection is a key tool. Assimilate your data, your thoughts, your feelings, your observations, your history, and turn it into learning. You know your strengths and your weaknesses—and seek feedback from others. Notice how your strengths and weaknesses and hopes and fears affect you and drive your choices. When important things happen, take time to notice your own feelings and responses. Notice the emotional responses and line of thought that it provokes. It's all data. Record these feelings. Junkies of this kind of thing use a reflective diary to capture all that stuff. It's not necessary, but some find it helpful.

Secondly, **do not fear change**, accept it as an opportunity to take action to live a diverse existence. Again, recognize your thoughts and feelings. Take note of the internal dialogue that goes on as you wrestle over decision making and fears of change. You can take learning from that. To develop is to change. It is in the nature of the journey.

Measure twice and cut once—it is always better to be safe than sorry.

Allow time for yourself. All of us, whether we are parents, children, husbands, wives, managers, coworkers, may sometimes feel blocked by the world around us. To learn is to accept a perfectly normal and shared experience. Following your own learning path sometimes means that you have to be selfish. Don't be afraid to take some "me time" when you need to. Recognize and satisfy your own needs. For many of us this is not as easy as it sounds. It can be hard to be selfish when others need you. But sometimes you have to be hard. To learn is to develop an appropriate level of assertiveness to enable you to hold a space for what needs to be done. Use the SPECTRUM model to help you. It works.

Love what you do. And if you don't love it, don't do it. Lots of things will catch your eye, but only a few catch your heart. Pursue those, talk about them passionately, and indulge your time on them. At the same time expect all your employees to love what they do, it is ok to have fun at work. Even undertakers and funeral directors have fun at work.

If you don't know something, just ask. You can learn a lot about yourself through feedback from others. You'd be surprised how many people will give you honest feedback if you ask the right way. Good questions such as "What did you think of the way I did X?" or "I'd like to get better at Y . . . could you suggest any changes I might make?" are all good ways of drawing out ideas from others. But then you must listen. Listen to the responses that others give to you, and if you don't understand it, or if you feel it's unclear, then simply ask them to clarify. Often, and I think this is especially true in organizations, we build up fantasies about why other people do what they do, or what type of lives they have, or how they think.

Sometimes we waste time tip-toeing softly around an issue that might not be real at all. You want to know if they think you're a good Project Manager? Just ask responsible questions. Step into your power. It sounds absurd, but its validity is proven.

Learn to be responsible. Sometimes we all feel that we can't get out of a situation. We might feel that things are being done to us to keep us in a less than perfect state. "I can't change that," for instance. Sometimes looking at it from a position of responsibility can help to determine a course of action. You can learn to change it.

Take a whole system focus and use Blood, Sweat and Tears We wrote these three volumes in the hope of helping others. It is our hope that we might assist a new business to start up, help an existing business review progress and for you as a team leader, manager, or leader to assist your own self-development. Be sure to read all three volumes of Blood, Sweat and Tears. Doing so should help you to ensure you don't overlook the things that many do; it should help you to ensure you are making a real profit, that as many of the stakeholders as possible are happy, you are in control and can easily move the business forward using simple tried and tested methods without confusion or fuss. It hasn't got everything in it you need, or it would be an encyclopedia, but it does contain our knowledge and wisdom, the knowledge of wisdom of our customers and their failures too—after all we learn more from our than we do successes.

You are now ready to read the final volume in our trilogy: Tears. Tears looks at:

Training: Are you developing yourself and others?

Encouragement: Do you know how to give encouragement to others and know where to find your own?

Announcements: Can you communicate effectively by announcing the right things and presenting them in the right way?

Review: Understand how you might best review the past and learn from it

Success: Can you use Blood, Sweat, and Tears to secure success for you, your team, and your business?

See you in the next book!

Index

OTHER TITLES IN THE ENTREPRENEURSHIP AND SMALL BUSINESS MANAGEMENT COLLECTION

Scott Shane, Case Western University, *Editor*

- *African American Entrepreneurs: Successes and Struggles of Entrepreneurs of Color in America* by Michelle Ingram Spain and J. Mark Munoz
- *How to Get Inside Someone's Mind and Stay There: The Small Business Owner's Guide to Content Marketing and Effective Message Creation* by Jacky Fitt
- *Profit: Plan for It, Get It—The Entrepreneurs Handbook* by H.R. Hutter
- *Navigating Entrepreneurship: 11 Proven Keys to Success* by Larry Jacobson
- *Global Women in the Start-up World: Conversations in Silicon Valley* by Marta Zucker
- *Understanding the Family Business: Exploring the Differences Between Family and Nonfamily Businesses, Second Edition* by Keanon J. Alderson
- *Growth-Oriented Entrepreneurship* by Alan S. Gutterman
- *Founders* by Alan S. Gutterman
- *Entrepreneurship* by Alan S. Gutterman
- *Sustainable Entrepreneurship* by Alan S. Gutterman
- *Startup Strategy Humor: Democratizing Startup Strategy* by Rajesh K. Pillania
- *Can You Run Your Business With Blood, Sweat, and Tears? Volume I: Blood* by Stephen Elkins-Jarrett and Nick Skinner
- *Can You Run Your Business With Blood, Sweat, and Tears? Volume III: Tear* by Stephen Elkins-Jarrett and Nick Skinner

Announcing the Business Expert Press Digital Library

Concise e-books business students need for classroom and research

This book can also be purchased in an e-book collection by your library as

- a one-time purchase,
- that is owned forever,
- allows for simultaneous readers,
- has no restrictions on printing, and
- can be downloaded as PDFs from within the library community.

Our digital library collections are a great solution to beat the rising cost of textbooks. E-books can be loaded into their course management systems or onto students' e-book readers.

The **Business Expert Press** digital libraries are very affordable, with no obligation to buy in future years. For more information, please visit **www.businessexpertpress.com/librarians**. To set up a trial in the United States, please email **sales@businessexpertpress.com**.